GOURMET
MADE
SIMPLE

GOURMET MADE SIMPLE

A Fresh Approach to Flavor
with Gena Knox

WRITTEN AND CREATED BY
GENA KNOX AND MARIE OSTROSKY
PHOTOGRAPHS BY ERICA GEORGE DINES

Library of Congress Catalog-In-Publication Data
is available by request.

ISBN   978-0-615-17548-5

Copyright © 2007 Fire & Flavor Grilling Co., Inc.®
Photographs copyright © 2007 Erica George Dines

Printed in China

PUBLISHED BY
Fire & Flavor Grilling Co., Inc.®
www.fireandflavor.com

DESIGNED AND PRODUCED BY
Ruffin Gillican, LLC
www.ruffingillican.com

PHOTOGRAPHS BY
Erica George Dines

FIRST EDITION

There is nothing more satisfying than sharing my passion for food and helping others take the challenge out of cooking. By pairing fresh ingredients with good food instincts and easy to follow recipes, preparing healthy, delicious meals will become fun and amazingly uncomplicated. *Gourmet Made Simple* can help you do just that.

—Gena Knox

CONTENTS

NOTES FROM THE CREATORS

GENA KNOX

Cookbooks and culinary magazines have always inspired me to create new dishes. But little did I know that my passion would take me from a career as a landscape architect into the world of culinary arts. After reading an article on the Native American tradition of plank grilling, I could not wait to try it at home. I purchased a couple of planks, keeping one to try out myself and giving the other to my mom — an amazing cook and a huge inspiration to me. We both planked salmon and came to the same conclusion: It was absolutely delicious and so simple to prepare.

I have now plank-grilled more food than you can imagine and still love every minute of it. After a long day at work, I cannot wait to get home, pour a glass of wine and start cooking. This book is filled with my favorite easy-to-follow recipes, proving that preparing healthy, delicious meals can be amazingly simple.

MARIE OSTROSKY

After spending 15 years as an audio engineer in TV and radio, I decided to follow my passion for cooking and attended culinary school. It was a decision that led to two years as Sting's private chef and the opportunity to cook and cater for other celebrities such as Martha Stewart. It was not until the start of a new career with the Food Network that I was able to combine both my culinary and production skills. At the time, the Food Network was in its infancy and I soon found myself working with many talented chefs and later as a producer on *Emeril Live*.

When I met Gena, I immediately loved her philosophy — it was such a simple approach to cooking. With her creativity, my background in communications, and our mutual love of cooking, I knew that we could create something wonderful.

MENU PLANNING *Rarely do I have several hours to prepare dinner, even when we are entertaining. Instead of making everything on the menu from scratch, I incorporate easy dishes or items purchased from the local market to save some time.*

ENTERTAINING

SPRING
Smoked Strawberry Mozzarella Crostini
Simple Salad with Green Goddess Dressing
Cedar-Wrapped Halibut with Fresh Vegetable Relish
Couscous
Chocolate Sorbet

SUMMER
Orange and Fennel-Marinated Olives
Fig and Arugula Salad
Maple Planked Snapper with Artichoke Pesto
Simple Roasted Potatoes
Frozen Lemon Meringue Pie

FALL
Butternut Squash Soup
Fresh Bread
Grilled Apple-Stuffed Pork Chops
Planked Green Beans with Blue Cheese
Sorbet and Prosecco Floats

WINTER
Apricot and Date Chutney Over Brie
Herb-Crusted Lamb Chops with Feta Topping
Cheese Polenta
Steamed Broccoli
Cappuccino Pots de Crème

WEEKNIGHT DINNERS

Cucumber Feta Salsa with Pita Chips

Cedar-Wrapped Salmon with Balsamic Glaze

Moroccan Couscous

Simple Roasted Asparagus

Drizzle asparagus with olive oil, salt, and pepper. Roast in a 400° oven
for 10 minutes. Top with fresh lemon juice and Parmesan cheese.

Skillet Spiced Nuts

Simple Green Salad

Toss mixed greens with cucumbers, tomatoes, Kalamata olives, and balsamic vinaigrette.

Prosciutto, Asparagus and Ricotta Pizza

Blue Cheese and Bacon Deviled Eggs

Apple, Parmesan and Mixed Green Salad

Rotisserie Chicken *(from local market)*

Sweet Potato Frites with Chipotle Aioli

Spinach Salad

Toss fresh spinach with cranberries, walnuts and goat cheese. Top with balsamic vinegar and olive oil.

Roasted Butternut Squash Soup

Turkey, Apple and Cheddar Open-faced Sandwich

Herb-Marinated Chicken with Artichoke-Tomato Salsa

Simple Roasted Potatoes

Sautéed Spinach

Sauté fresh spinach with olive oil and garlic. Finish with lemon juice and Parmesan cheese.

Bourbon-Marinated Flank Steak

Grilled Vegetables

Cheese Polenta

WEEKEND DINNERS

Marinated Bocconcini
Southern Peach Salad with Toasted Pecans
Planked Prosciutto-Wrapped Swordfish Skewers
Chipotle Mashed Sweet Potatoes
Watermelon Basil Granita

Marinated Fig and Arugula Salad
Mediterranean Stuffed Chicken Breasts
Simple Roasted Potatoes
Jewel's Fruit Cobbler

Simple Salad with Green Goddess Dressing
Shrimp B.L.T. Tacos
Black-Bean Cakes
Cranberry and White Chocolate Chip Cookies

Herbed Goat Cheese Log
Grilled Pork Tenderloin with Sweet Onion Sauce
Maple-Planked Green Beans
Moroccan Couscous

Watermelon, Feta and Arugula Salad
Olive Lamb Burger with Mint Gremolata
Mustard Herb Potato Salad
Simple Fudge Cakes

Shrimp and Mango Summer Rolls
Asian Chicken Burgers with Cucumber Slaw
Peanut Soba Noodles
Chocolate Sorbet

PAIRING FOOD WITH WINE

Matching food and wine is a matter of individual taste.
The best approach is to consult your local wine store; they are the experts and love to help.

Beginning a meal with a light, appetizer-friendly wine is always a good idea. You can find almost all of these choices for under $10, and they'll taste like they cost $50. Plank-grilled foods take on an extra layer of flavor, which gives you more versatility when pairing wines. White wine, for instance, is not always the choice for planked seafood or chicken; their rich smoky flavors match perfectly with light- to medium-bodied reds and heavier white wines.

PROSECCO Italian sparkling wine
CAVA Spanish sparkling wine
CHAMPAGNE French sparkling wine (generally a little more expensive)
SPARKLING WINE United States, South America, New Zealand, Canada and Australia
VINHO VERDE Semi-sparkling wine from Portugal (the perfect summer wine)

TEMPERATURE TIPS
Whether the wine you are serving is $10 or $60, the proper temperature makes a substantial difference in its flavor.

WHITE WINES SHOULD BE SERVED AT 55°, WHICH CAN BE ACHIEVED BY STORING

In a refrigerator	1½ hours
In a freezer	40 minutes
In ice water with ⅓ cup salt	8 minutes

RED WINE SHOULD BE SERVED AT 65°, WHICH CAN BE ACHIEVED BY STORING

| In a refrigerator | 20 minutes |

NOTE *If red wine has been stored in the refrigerator longer than 1½ hours,*
let it sit at room temperature 20 minutes before serving.

STORING AN OPENED BOTTLE OF WINE
Use a rubber stopper to prevent the wine from being exposed to air.
Store red and white wines in the refrigerator; this will prolong the life of a wine by about 2 days.
For sparking wines use a champagne stopper, which will keep the wine bubbly for an extra day or two.

TOOLS OF THE TRADE

With time and accuracy being of the essence in cooking,
having the right equipment will make you a happier and more effective cook.
Along with the basics, here are some tools every kitchen should have.

GOOD KNIVES A good set of knives is an investment, but also a must. If you prefer, build your set one at a time. Start with a chef's knife and then add a paring knife, a serrated tomato knife and a bread knife. Good, sharp knives make cooking less stressful.

MICROPLANE OR ZESTER Either of these tools makes zesting an orange, lemon or lime quick and easy. Remember: Use only the colored part of the zest; the white pith has a bitter flavor.

RUBBER SPATULAS Large spatulas are perfect for removing the last drop of batter from a mixing bowl or stirring any type of dish. Mini spatulas are great when removing liquids from small bowls or measuring cups, and they are heat-proof.

CARROT PEELER This versatile tool can be used for so much more than peeling carrots. Use it to peel potatoes, apples, and asparagus spears and even to shave hard cheeses like Parmesan.

KITCHEN SHEARS A good pair of kitchen shears is invaluable for cutting flower stems, chicken bones, herbs and so much more.

STACK OF MIXING BOWLS A graduated set of bowls is useful for all types of cooking. The smallest sizes work perfectly for mixing rubs or arranging prepped ingredients.

GRILL PAN When the weather is not suitable for outdoor grilling, a grill pan is an essential (see Resources, page 184).

HAND EMULSION BLENDER This inexpensive device makes pureeing soups easy, saves you of time, and is easy to clean.

MINI WHISK When mixing dressings or marinades in small bowls, a mini whisk is easy to handle.

DEVELOPING GOOD FOOD INSTINCTS

Cooking is fun and can be less complicated if you have fresh ingredients,
easy-to-follow recipes and good food instincts.

SEASON WITH SALT AS YOU COOK To add layers of flavor to any dish, add a pinch of salt at the start of the cooking process, another halfway through, and a final one at the end.

MAKE A RECIPE YOUR OWN Don't be afraid to experiment with ingredients or to substitute if you don't have certain ingredients on hand. Consider replacing goat cheese with feta, romaine with arugula, pecans with walnuts; the list is virtually endless. Likewise, flavored vinegars and oils can add an extra burst of flavor; try replacing balsamic with raspberry vinegar or olive oil with walnut oil.

LEARN TO PEEL GARLIC THE EASY WAY Place the flat side of a chef's knife on top of a garlic clove, with the blade pointed away from you. Make a fist with your free hand and give the knife a quick pound. You'll crush the garlic, which will cause the peeling to come right off.

USE FRESH HERBS Basil, rosemary, thyme and mint are some of my favorites, but any fresh herbs will make a dish stand out. If they look a little limp when you take them out of the refrigerator, trim off the tips of the stems and submerge the herbs in cold water for 10 minutes and they'll perk right up.

MAKE YOUR OWN SALAD DRESSING Taking a few extra minutes to whip up a fresh dressing makes all the difference.

CUT DOWN ON OIL When using a marinade or salad-dressing recipe that calls for quite a bit of oil, substitute half the amount with vegetable or chicken broth to create a healthier dish.

USE CITRUS ZEST FOR EXTRA FLAVOR A teaspoon of lime, orange or lemon zest will brighten salad dressings, marinades, meats, even rice and pasta.

LEARN GOOD KNIFE SKILLS Take a class at your local cooking school or gourmet store to learn the basics of how to cut an onion and other everyday foods. You'll not only minimize the chances of cutting yourself, you'll save time in the kitchen.

ESSENTIAL KITCHEN SKILLS

BLANCHING VEGETABLES *Green beans, snow peas, asparagus, broccoli, Brussels sprouts and carrots are perfect candidates for blanching, a cooking method that preserves the vegetable's color, flavor and texture.* Blanch vegetables before sautéing to ensure the perfect dish. Boil vegetables in salted water for 3 to 4 minutes or until they are brightly colored and crisp tender. While vegetables are steaming, fill a large bowl with ice water. Immediately strain vegetables through a colander and submerge in ice water until they are no longer warm to the touch. Drain and dry with paper towels.

REHYDRATING SUN-DRIED TOMATOES *You can purchase sun-dried tomatoes packed dry and simply rehydrate them yourself.* Place dried tomatoes in a microwave-safe dish. Add enough water to fill two inches above tomatoes. Microwave on high for 2 minutes, then let rest 15 minutes or until tomatoes are soft and plump.

SEGMENTING AN ORANGE *Orange and grapefruit segments are delicious in salads and salsas, and the technique is incredibly easy.* Slice off both ends of the orange or grapefruit with a small serrated knife. Stand the fruit on the flat bottom and slice down the sides, removing the peel in strips. Remove as much white pith as possible without sacrificing too much of the fruit. Hold orange or grapefruit over a bowl and run your knife between each membrane, cutting the segments free so they fall into the bowl with the juices.

MAKING STORE-BOUGHT STOCK TASTE HOMEMADE *Although homemade stock is delicious, I rarely have time to make it.* To add extra flavor to stock-based soups, simply infuse the store-bought variety with spices, vegetables and herbs. Warm stock over medium heat. Stir in your favorite herbs and spices and simmer 20 minutes. Strain stock and use in your favorite soups and stews.

RECOMMENDED FLAVOR COMBINATIONS

    ASIAN — infuse with cilantro, black peppercorns and 3 quarter-size slices of fresh ginger.

    BASIC HERB — thyme, parsley, rosemary, 2 thin lemon slices and black peppercorns.

    ITALIAN — fresh oregano, Parmesan cheese rind, garlic and black peppercorns.

ROASTED BELL PEPPERS *While you can purchase peppers already roasted, it's easy to do it yourself; the color and texture of freshly roasted peppers is always a nice touch to a meal.* **How to:** Preheat oven to 500°. Cut peppers in half, starting from the stem at the top and working down. Remove seeds and white interior; place cut side down on a cookie sheet lined with foil. Bake 8 minutes or until the skin of the peppers are mostly black. Remove from the oven, then gather the foil around the peppers and seal so no heat can escape. Allow to rest 5 minutes; uncover and let cool. The blistered skins of the peppers will peel off easily. Chop and serve with pastas, appetizers, or in salads and salsas.

CHAPTER ONE | Appetizers

ROASTED BUTTERNUT SQUASH SOUP

Perfect for fall, this soup can easily be made ahead and put in the freezer. The Serrano chile gives the dish a hint of heat, but it's perfectly balanced by the sour cream garnish.

PLACE indoor
PREP TIME 15 minutes
COOK TIME 40 minutes
YIELD 6 appetizer or 4 main course servings

1 three-pound butternut squash
2 tablespoons olive oil, divided
½ medium onion, chopped
3 cloves garlic, minced
1 Serrano chile, seeded and minced
1 tablespoon grated fresh ginger
⅛ teaspoon cayenne pepper
2 cups chicken or vegetable stock
½ tablespoon brown sugar
Sour cream to garnish

FIRST Preheat oven to 425°. Cut squash in half, horizontally, and remove seeds. Rub outside of squash with 1 tablespoon olive oil and place face down on a baking sheet lined with parchment paper. Roast for 30 minutes or until squash is almost tender; remove from oven and cool. Peel squash and cut into 2-inch cubes; set aside.

NEXT In a large stock pot, heat remaining olive oil over medium-high heat. Sauté onions, garlic and chile for 3 to 4 minutes or until slightly brown, adding a pinch of salt as you cook. Stir in ginger and cayenne pepper and cook for one more minute. Add cubed squash, stock and brown sugar; bring to a boil. Cover, reduce heat and simmer for 10 minutes, or until the squash is very tender.

LAST Purée soup with a handheld emulsifier or, working in batches, a blender or food processor. Return soup to pot and add additional stock or milk, if needed, to achieve desired consistency. Season with salt and pepper and garnish each bowl with 1 tablespoon of sour cream.

CHILLED AVOCADO SOUP WITH SMOKY TOMATOES

This creamy but light soup is a great dinner complement to plank-grilled salmon. Because the servings are generous, you may want to save a little for lunch the next day.

PLACE indoor
PREP TIME 10 minutes
COOK TIME 10 minutes
YIELD 4 servings

SOUP

2 ripe avocados, diced
½ English cucumber, diced
½ medium onion, chopped
1 lemon, zested and juiced
1 cup low-fat buttermilk
2 cups chicken stock
Cayenne pepper

SMOKY TOMATOES

20 cherry or pear tomatoes
1 15-inch cedar grilling plank, soaked

FIRST Preheat grill to medium-low heat. Place soaked plank on grill, close lid and heat 3 minutes. Turn plank over with tongs, place tomatoes on heated side (or in grill basket atop plank) and grill, with lid closed, 8 to 10 minutes or until tomatoes begin to blister and burst. Remove tomatoes and plank from grill; season tomatoes with salt and pepper and set aside.

LAST Combine avocados, cucumber, onion, lemon zest and lemon juice in a blender or food processor. Pour in buttermilk and purée. Add stock, one cup at a time, until the soup is creamy but not too thick; season to taste with salt, black pepper and cayenne pepper. Spoon soup into bowls (one cup each) and top with smoky tomatoes.

FIRE-ROASTED TOMATO SOUP

This soup gets its rich flavor from fire-roasting the tomatoes
on a grill and is delicious served hot or cold.

PLACE indoor/outdoor
PREP TIME soak + 10 minutes
COOK TIME 40 minutes
YIELD 6 servings

3 medium tomatoes
2 tablespoons olive oil
1 medium onion, chopped
1 tablespoon minced garlic
2 cups chicken stock
2 cups fresh basil leaves
1 14½-ounce can diced tomatoes
½ teaspoon salt

FIRST Preheat grill to medium-low heat. Slice the tomatoes into eighths and place on a sheet of heavy-duty aluminum foil. Grill tomatoes 12 to 15 minutes, until they release their juices and the skins begin to curl. While tomatoes are grilling, heat the olive oil in a 4-quart sauce pan. Sauté onions 10 to 12 minutes, or until they start to brown.

NEXT Mix garlic with onions and sauté another 15 seconds, then add grilled tomatoes (with juices that have been released), chicken stock, basil, canned tomatoes, and salt. Bring to a boil, then reduce heat and simmer for 25 minutes.

LAST Once the soup has simmered, purée with an immersion blender, food processor or beverage blender. If using a food processor or blender, allow soup to slightly cool first.

NOTE To roast tomatoes in the oven, heat the oven to 350°; roast for 20 minutes or until the tomatoes begin to soften and slightly blister.

BLUE CHEESE AND BACON DEVILED EGGS

This is a delicious spin on a favorite Southern treat.
Be sure to make extras; these are always a crowd pleaser.

PLACE indoor
PREP TIME 15 minutes
COOK TIME 10 minutes
YIELD 4 servings

4 eggs
2 teaspoons mayonnaise
1 teaspoon Dijon mustard
2 slices cooked bacon, crumbled and divided
1½ tablespoons crumbled blue cheese
1 teaspoon chopped fresh parsley

FIRST Place eggs in large pot in a single layer. Add cold water, covering the eggs by an inch. Bring the water to a boil; cover and remove from heat. After 10 minutes, drain and run cool water over the eggs. Allow to cool, then peel and halve lengthwise.

NEXT Place yolks in a medium bowl; using a fork, mash with mayonnaise and mustard. Stir in half of the crumbled bacon, the blue cheese and parsley until combined. Season with salt and freshly ground black pepper.

LAST Spoon the mixture into egg halves and top with remaining bacon pieces.

SMOKED STRAWBERRY MOZZARELLA CROSTINI

Don't be daunted by the fact that this appetizer is planked;
it's well worth the extra 10 minutes. The combination of strawberries,
balsamic vinegar and smoky cheese is amazing.

PLACE indoor/outdoor
PREP TIME soak + 10 minutes
COOK TIME 10 minutes
YIELD 4 servings

1½ cups fresh strawberries, sliced

1 tablespoon balsamic vinegar

1 teaspoon sugar

1 8-ounce ball fresh mozzarella,
   packed in water, sliced ½ inch thick

8 baguette slices, ½ inch thick and
   toasted in oven or on grill

1 15-inch cedar or alder grilling plank, soaked

8 large basil leaves

FIRST Preheat grill to medium-low heat. In a small bowl, combine strawberries, balsamic vinegar and sugar; set aside to marinate. Place soaked plank on grill, close lid and allow to heat for 3 minutes. Using tongs, turn plank over and place baguette slices on the heated side.

NEXT Top each baguette slice with mozzarella; close the lid and grill for 8 to 10 minutes, or until cheese melts and edges begin to brown.

LAST Remove plank and baguette slices from grill. Add one basil leaf and marinated strawberries to each slice. Serve immediately.

NOTE For indoor preparation, place the cheese-topped crostini in 400° oven for 7 minutes or until the cheese melts.

SHRIMP AND MANGO SUMMER ROLLS

Even if you've never made summer rolls before, this recipe is a snap.
Once you assemble the ingredients, the rest is easy. Serve them as appetizers
with sparkling wine, or with Peanut Soba Noodles (page 133) for a light dinner.

PLACE indoor
PREP TIME 25 minutes
YIELD 4 servings

SUMMER ROLLS

8 large shrimp, cooked and peeled,
  halved lengthwise

8 round rice paper rolls (8-inch diameter)

4 butter lettuce leaves,
  halved with ribs removed

½ English cucumber,
  cut into matchstick-size strips

½ mango, cut into matchstick-size strips

½ avocado, thinly sliced

½ cup shredded carrots

¼ cup mint leaves, roughly chopped

¼ cup loosely packed cilantro leaves

DIPPING SAUCE

2½ tablespoons mirin (sweet rice wine)

2 tablespoons soy sauce

2 tablespoons rice vinegar

1 tablespoon green onions, thinly sliced

½ Serrano chile, thinly sliced

FIRST Combine sauce ingredients in a small bowl and set aside. Fill a pie plate with 1 inch of water; set next to work surface. One at a time, submerge each wrapper in water for 30 seconds, or until it becomes pliable. Transfer the rice paper to your work surface. Place a lettuce leaf over the bottom third of the rice paper; top the lettuce with 3 strips each of cucumber, mango and avocado. Finish with ½ tablespoon carrots.

LAST Starting from the bottom, roll up the paper halfway; fold both sides of paper in toward filling. Place 2 shrimp halves, cut sides down and end-to-end, along the crease. Add 1 teaspoon each cilantro and mint leaves over the shrimp. Continue to roll the rice paper into a cylinder, pressing the edges to seal. Place roll, seam side down, on a plate and cover with a damp towel. Repeat with remaining rolls; serve with dipping sauce.

NOTE This appetizer can be prepared up to 3 hours ahead of time. Wrap each roll with a damp paper towel, put on a plate and cover with plastic wrap. Store in the refrigerator until ready to use.

CEDAR-WRAPPED MUSHROOMS WITH GOAT CHEESE

Mushrooms are a perfect match for cedar papers;
they soak up the subtle smoky flavor. For a quick meal,
toss the warm mushrooms and cheese with your favorite pasta.

PLACE indoor/outdoor
PREP TIME 15 minutes
COOK TIME 8 minutes
YIELD 4 servings

2 large Portobello mushroom caps,
   cleaned and sliced ½ inch thick
12 ¼-inch strips roasted red bell pepper
3 tablespoons balsamic vinegar
1 tablespoon olive oil
1 teaspoon fresh thyme leaves
¼ cup crumbled goat cheese
4 6x6-inch cedar grilling papers, soaked
Cotton string for tying

FIRST In a large bowl, toss mushroom slices with vinegar, oil and thyme leaves; season with salt and pepper. Let marinate at room temperature 10 minutes.

NEXT Preheat grill or grill pan to medium heat. Divide seasoned mushrooms and red pepper strips equally; place on cedar papers and top with crumbled goat cheese. Fold edges of cedar papers toward each other, overlapping the edges and tying with the cotton string, if necessary.

LAST Place mushroom rolls on grill and cook 4 minutes per side or until tender. Remove from grill with tongs and serve immediately with fresh bread.

CUCUMBER FETA SALSA

This simple appetizer is great with pita chips,
but it's also a tasty topping for cedar-planked salmon and grilled tuna.

PLACE indoor
PREP TIME 10 minutes
YIELD 2½ cups

1 large English cucumber, diced
½ large red onion, diced
3 ounces feta cheese, crumbled
¼ cup chopped Kalamata olives (optional)
1 lemon, juiced
2 tablespoons chopped fresh mint

FIRST Combine all the ingredients in a medium bowl. Season with salt and pepper to taste; mix well. Serve with pita chips.

WARM BRIE WITH APRICOT AND DATE CHUTNEY

This chutney is just as delicious served with goat cheese on top of crostini. It's a versatile accompaniment, even served as part of a main course with grilled pork or duck.

PLACE indoor
PREP TIME 10 minutes
COOK TIME 20 minutes
YIELD 8 servings

¾ cup dried apricots, chopped
¾ cup dried dates, chopped
1 cup chopped onion
½ cup apple cider vinegar
½ cup brown sugar
1 teaspoon grated fresh ginger
1 teaspoon tomato paste
¼ teaspoon cinnamon
¼ teaspoon red pepper flakes
2 tablespoons chopped fresh
   parsley (plus extra for garnish)
8- to 10-ounce round of brie,
   top rind removed

FIRST Place apricots and dates in a microwave-safe bowl; add 2 cups water and microwave on high 2 minutes. Allow apricots and dates to rehydrate in the hot water for an additional 5 minutes. Drain.

NEXT In a medium saucepan, combine apricots, dates, onion, vinegar, sugar, ginger, tomato paste, cinnamon and red pepper. Bring to a boil; reduce heat and simmer for 15 minutes, stirring occasionally. Stir in parsley.

LAST While chutney is simmering, preheat oven to 350°. Place brie on baking sheet, cut side up; bake 10 minutes, or until soft. Transfer to serving platter and top with desired amount of chutney. Garnish with extra parsley and serve with fresh bread or crackers.

ORANGE AND
FENNEL MARINATED OLIVES

Delicious with manchego cheese, these olives take only 5 minutes to make.

PLACE indoor
PREP TIME 10 minutes
YIELD 2½ cups

2 cups assorted olives
¾ cup fennel, thinly sliced
½ cup extra virgin olive oil
2 tablespoons white wine vinegar
3 tablespoons orange zest
¼ teaspoon red pepper flakes
3 orange slices, very thin

FIRST Rinse olives under running water; drain. In a medium saucepan, combine olives and remaining ingredients. Cook over low heat 5 minutes; remove from heat and allow to marinate at least 5 minutes before serving. Serve warm or at room temperature.

NOTE These olives will keep for up to a week in the refrigerator, but be sure to bring them to room temperature before serving. For more intense flavor, allow olives to marinate for an hour.

FIVE-MINUTE APPETIZERS

For last-minute entertaining or just a satisfying snack, these quick treats will be sure to impress.

PROSCIUTTO AND MELON

Use a melon baller to cut spheres of cantaloupe, honeydew or watermelon. Wrap each ball with a thin strip of prosciutto; slide the prosciutto-wrapped melon onto 4-inch skewers, about 3 balls per skewer. (In place of prosciutto, you can also use thinly sliced, air-cured ham such as Serrano.) As a finishing touch, grind cracked black pepper over the appetizer or add a sprinkle of either chopped basil or mint.

MARINATED BOCCONCINI

In a medium bowl, combine ½ cup olive oil with 2 tablespoons of capers, 1 tablespoon chopped fresh oregano, the zest of 1 lemon and a few grinds of black pepper. (Or use chopped parsley, 1 whole peeled clove of garlic and a pinch of red pepper flakes for spicier flavor.) Pour over 8 ounces of bocconcini; toss to coat and serve. If making ahead of time, store in the refrigerator; before serving, bring to room temperature.

SKILLET SPICED NUTS

In a skillet, heat 2 tablespoons of olive oil with your favorite dried herbs or spices. Try rosemary and oregano for a Mediterranean flavor or spice things up with a combination of cumin, cinnamon and cayenne. Let the oil infuse with the herbs approximately 15 seconds, then toss in a cup of your favorite nuts and toast for 3 to 4 minutes, or until you smell a toasted, nutty aroma. Transfer to a plate and sprinkle with salt while still warm.

HERBED GOAT CHEESE

Finely chop ¼ cup of your favorite fresh herbs, such as parsley, basil or tarragon. Roll an 11-ounce log of fresh goat cheese in the herb mixture, coating it all the way around. Arrange the cheese log on a platter with crackers, apple wedges or slices of baguette bread. In lieu of fresh herbs, you can also use cracked black pepper, smoked paprika, lemon zest or finely chopped nuts.

CHAPTER TWO | Salads

APPLE, PARMESAN AND MIXED GREEN SALAD WITH MUSTARD VINAIGRETTE

The combination of these ingredients makes a beautiful salad.
Use the best-quality Parmesan you can find; it makes a world of difference.

PLACE indoor
PREP TIME 10 minutes
YIELD 4 servings

SALAD
5 cups mixed greens
1 Braeburn or Gala apple, thinly sliced
⅓ cup walnuts, lightly toasted
½ cup Parmesan cheese curls

DRESSING
1 tablespoon whole grain mustard
1 tablespoon water
1 tablespoon honey
1½ tablespoons sherry vinegar
2 tablespoons olive oil

FIRST Combine the dressing ingredients in a small bowl. Season with salt and pepper; set aside.

LAST In a large salad bowl, combine greens, apples and walnuts; toss with dressing. Add Parmesan curls and gently toss to combine. Serve immediately.

PLANKED PORTOBELLO PANZANELLA

This salad takes a little longer to make but it's worth the extra effort.
Crumbled blue cheese or feta can be substituted for the Parmesan cheese.

PLACE indoor/outdoor
PREP TIME 10 minutes
COOK TIME 20 minutes
YIELD 4 servings

SALAD

3 cups ciabatta or French bread, cubed
1 large clove garlic, minced
4 tablespoons olive oil, divided
½ cup red onion, thinly sliced
3 cups tomatoes, coarsely chopped
2 tablespoons red wine vinegar
½ cup fresh basil, leaves torn
Parmesan cheese curls (optional)

MUSHROOMS

2 tablespoons balsamic vinegar
1 tablespoon olive oil
4 large portobello caps,
   cleaned and stems removed
1 15-inch cedar, alder or maple
   grilling plank, soaked

FIRST Preheat grill to medium low. Combine balsamic vinegar and 1 tablespoon of olive oil in a gallon-size zip-top bag; add mushroom caps and gently toss to coat. Place plank on grill and heat for 3 minutes. Turn plank over and place mushrooms caps, bottom sides up, on plank. Close lid and cook 12 to 15 minutes or until mushrooms are slightly tender. Remove mushrooms and plank from grill; loosely tent mushrooms with aluminum foil.

NEXT While mushrooms are cooking, toss bread cubes with minced garlic and 2 tablespoons of olive oil. Place on a cookie sheet, in a single layer. Bake 15 minutes or until bread is lightly toasted.

LAST In a large salad bowl, combine onions, tomatoes, vinegar and remaining 2 tablespoons of olive oil; season with salt and pepper to taste. Add bread cubes and fresh basil leaves; toss to coat. Place mushrooms caps, bottom side up, on 4 plates and top with equal portions of the salad mixture. Sprinkle with Parmesan curls, if desired. Serve immediately.

NOTE The mushrooms can also be baked, without a plank, in a 350° oven for 10 minutes, or until slightly tender.

POMEGRANATE, AVOCADO AND ORANGE SALAD

This salad adapts well to any fresh fruit and cheese. If pomegranates aren't in season, use dried cranberries for the extra splash of color.

PLACE indoor
PREP TIME 10 minutes
YIELD 4 servings

SALAD

5 cups mixed greens
2 navel oranges, segmented
2 ounces feta cheese, crumbled
1 avocado, thinly sliced
Seeds of ½ pomegranate

DRESSING

1 orange, juiced
1 tablespoon rice vinegar
1 tablespoon olive oil
½ tablespoon maple syrup
½ tablespoon Dijon mustard
1 tablespoon water

FIRST Combine dressing ingredients in a small bowl. Season with salt and pepper; set aside.

LAST In large salad bowl, combine mixed greens and orange segments; lightly toss with enough dressing to coat. Add feta cheese and avocado; gently toss again. Divide the salad among 4 plates and top with pomegranate seeds. Leftover dressing can be stored in the refrigerator for up to 3 days.

SIMPLE SALAD WITH
GREEN GODDESS DRESSING

Use your leftover dressing to marinate grilled chicken or as a sauce for fish tacos.

PLACE indoor
PREP TIME 10 minutes
YIELD 4 servings

SALAD

2 large vine-ripened tomatoes,
   cut into wedges
5 cups mixed greens

DRESSING

¼ cup plain yogurt
⅓ cup mayonnaise
¼ cup mint leaves, loosely packed
¼ cup cilantro leaves, loosely packed
1 large clove garlic
½-inch piece of ginger, peeled
2 tablespoons fresh lime juice
1 tablespoon honey
2 tablespoons olive oil

FIRST Combine the dressing ingredients in a blender; purée and refrigerate.

LAST Divide greens among 4 plates; top each with tomato wedges and 2 tablespoons dressing. Serve immediately.

WATERMELON, FETA AND ARUGULA SALAD

The inspiration for this salad came from one of my favorite chefs, Hugh Acheson, from the Five and Ten Restaurant near our house in Athens, Georgia.

PLACE indoor
PREP TIME 10 minutes
YIELD 4 servings

SALAD

3 cups arugula
4 cups watermelon, cubed
½ cup red onion, thinly sliced
¾ cup feta cheese, cubed

DRESSING

¼ cup fresh lime juice
1 tablespoon rice vinegar
1 teaspoon granulated sugar
2 tablespoons fresh mint, finely chopped
2 teaspoons jalapeño, seeded and minced
½ cup olive oil

FIRST To make dressing, whisk lime juice, vinegar, sugar, mint, jalapeño and oil in a small bowl. Season with salt and pepper to taste.

LAST In a large serving bowl, combine watermelon, arugula, red onion, and feta cheese. Toss with dressing and then serve immediately.

SOUTHERN PEACH SALAD
WITH TOASTED PECANS

While growing up in Georgia, my job every summer was to sell peaches.
As a result, my mom and I came up with countless recipes using
the fresh fruit, and this is her favorite. If you like a lighter dressing,
substitute half of the oil with vegetable or chicken stock.

PLACE indoor
PREP TIME 10 minutes
YIELD 4 servings

SALAD
2 peaches, cut into 8 wedges each
5 cups baby spinach leaves
2 ounces goat cheese, crumbled

DRESSING
3 tablespoons balsamic vinegar
1 tablespoon fresh lemon juice
1 tablespoon honey
½ tablespoon Dijon mustard
½ cup olive oil
1 small shallot, minced

SPICED PECANS
3 teaspoons sugar
⅛ teaspoon allspice
¼ teaspoon red pepper flakes
⅓ cup pecan halves

FIRST To make spiced pecans, combine sugar, allspice and red pepper in a small bowl; set aside. In a small skillet, toast pecans over low heat for 5 minutes or until lightly toasted, stirring frequently. Sprinkle with sugar mixture and cook one more minute, stirring constantly. Remove pecans from skillet and spread on waxed paper to cool.

NEXT In a large bowl, whisk together dressing ingredients; season with salt and pepper. In a separate bowl, toss peaches, salad greens and pecans with enough vinaigrette to coat.

LAST Divide salad among four salad plates; top with goat cheese and then serve. Any leftover dressing will keep in the refrigerator for up to 3 days.

GRILLED CAESAR SALAD WITH SUN-DRIED TOMATO DRESSING

A fresh new blend of classic flavors. I always make a little extra dressing to toss with grilled vegetables.

PLACE indoor/outdoor
PREP TIME 10 minutes
COOK TIME 5 minutes
YIELD 4 servings

SALAD

4 hearts of romaine lettuce
Baguette slices, toasted on grill or in oven
1 large clove garlic

DRESSING

4 sun-dried tomato halves
   (not packed in oil)
1 cup boiling water
1 tablespoon balsamic vinegar
1 tablespoon fresh lemon juice
1 clove garlic
1 teaspoon sugar
½ teaspoon anchovy paste
   (or one anchovy, patted dry)
3 tablespoons olive oil
1 ounce finely grated Parmesan cheese

FIRST Pre-heat grill to medium heat. Cut hearts of romaine in half, lengthwise, and set aside. Slice garlic clove in half; rub exposed end onto each toasted baguette slice and set aside.

NEXT Bring the water to a boil in a pan; place the sun-dried tomatoes in the boiling water and remove pan from heat. Wait 5 minutes for the tomatoes to rehydrate. Remove tomatoes from water, reserving the water for later use. In a food processor, combine rehydrated tomatoes, vinegar, lemon juice, garlic, sugar, anchovy paste and 3 tablespoons of tomato liquid. Purée while slowly drizzling in olive oil. Add more tomato water (1 to 2 tablespoons) until the desired consistency is reached. Season the dressing with salt and pepper.

LAST Place lettuce halves, cut side down, on grill and cook for 2 to 3 minutes, until grill marks start to form. Remove from grill and transfer to platter. Drizzle dressing over grilled hearts, top with Parmesan cheese and serve with baguette slices on the side.

MARINATED FIG AND ARUGULA SALAD

This recipe transforms simple ingredients—and techniques—into a spectacular salad.

PLACE indoor
PREP TIME 10 minutes
YIELD 4 servings

1 large shallot, minced
2 tablespoons balsamic vinegar
2 tablespoons olive oil
1 tablespoon vegetable stock
1 teaspoon honey
12 fresh figs, halved
5 cups arugula
3 ounces blue cheese, crumbled

FIRST In a large bowl, whisk together the shallot, vinegar, oil, vegetable stock and honey; season with salt and pepper. Add halved figs and let marinate for 10 minutes.

LAST Toss the marinated figs with arugula and blue cheese. Serve immediately.

CHAPTER THREE | Fresh Fast Food

TURKEY, APPLE AND CHEDDAR OPEN-FACED SANDWICH

This sandwich, with Butternut Squash Soup (page 27), makes a simple but hearty meal. If your crowd is extra-hungry, you may want to double the recipe.

PLACE indoor
PREP TIME 5 minutes
COOK TIME 5 minutes
YIELD 4 servings

SANDWICH

4 large slices ciabatta bread,
   cut ½ inch thick and toasted
12 ounces smoked turkey
1 Granny Smith apple, halved,
   cored, and sliced thin
4 1-ounce slices cheddar cheese

APPLE SPREAD

½ cup apple butter
¼ cup Dijon mustard

FIRST Preheat oven 500°. Combine apple butter and mustard in a small bowl. Spread 1½ tablespoons onto each piece of bread and top with 3 ounces of turkey. Layer apple slices on top of the turkey and finish with cheese.

LAST Bake just until the cheese melts and the edges begin to brown, about 3 minutes.

OLIVE LAMB BURGER WITH MINT GREMOLATA

This burger, a fresh new twist on the combination of lamb and mint, will have your guests clamoring for more. Try the mint gremolata with lamb chops, salmon or grilled tuna.

PLACE indoor/outdoor
PREP TIME 15 minutes
COOK TIME 10 minutes
YIELD 4 servings

BURGERS

1½ pounds ground lamb
⅓ cup chopped and pitted
   kalamata olives
1 teaspoon dried oregano
4 hamburger buns

GREMOLATA

½ cup chopped fresh mint
¼ cup chopped flat-leaf parsley
2 cloves garlic, minced
1 large lemon, grated zest and juiced
2 tablespoons olive oil

FIRST Prepare grill or grill pan to medium-hot. To make the sauce, combine mint, parsley, garlic, lemon juice and zest, and oil. Season with salt and pepper and set aside.

NEXT In a large bowl, combine lamb, olives, and oregano; season with a generous amount of black pepper and a touch of salt. Divide the mixture into 4 equal patties, about ½ inch thick.

LAST Cook the burgers until seared on one side, about 3 to 4 minutes. Flip the burgers and continue cooking, about 4 minutes for medium, or until desired doneness. Serve with gremolata sauce.

PLANKED BLUE CHEESE BURGER

This is the burger we traditionally serve on Memorial Day—
and our guests can't get enough. The planks give these burgers extra flavor,
but you can just as easily grill them without a plank.

PLACE indoor/outdoor
PREP TIME soak + 10 minutes
COOK TIME 15 minutes
YIELD 4 servings

1½ pounds ground beef
¾ cup blue cheese crumbles
½ jalapeño, minced (or more to taste)
Salt and pepper
1 15-inch cedar grilling plank, soaked
4 hamburger buns
Lettuce and tomato for garnish

FIRST Preheat grill to high. Combine ground beef with blue cheese and jalapeño; season with salt and pepper. Form 4 patties, about 1 inch thick.

NEXT Sear burgers 1 to 2 minutes per side; remove from grill. Place burgers on a plate and cover with aluminum foil.

LAST Lower heat to medium-low and place plank on grill. Close lid and heat plank 3 minutes. Turn the plank over and place seared burgers on heated side; close the grill's lid and cook for 10 minutes (for medium-well). Remove plank and burgers from grill; serve with buns and additional toppings.

NOTE To cook the burgers without a plank, preheat a grill or grill pan to medium-high heat; cook for 4 minutes per side for medium-rare, or until desired doneness.

ASIAN CHICKEN BURGERS
WITH CUCUMBER SLAW

These burgers are perfect if you prefer something a little lighter than beef.

PLACE indoor/outdoor
PREP TIME soak + 20 minutes
COOK TIME 20 minutes
YIELD 4 servings

BURGERS

1½ pounds ground chicken

½ cup purchased teriyaki sauce
  (for homemade recipe, see page 97)

1 tablespoon toasted sesame oil

4 large scallions, halved and thinly sliced

¼ cup chopped fresh basil

¼ cup chopped fresh cilantro

2 tablespoons chopped fresh mint

1 15-inch maple or alder plank, soaked

4 hamburger buns, toasted

CUCUMBER SLAW

¾ cup rice wine vinegar

1 tablespoon sugar

2 teaspoons kosher salt

½ English cucumber, cut into ¼-inch slices

½ small white onion, halved and sliced

½ small Serrano pepper, thinly sliced

1 tablespoon chopped fresh mint

1½ tablespoons sesame seeds

FIRST In a small saucepan, combine rice vinegar, sugar and salt; cook over medium heat until dissolved, about 3 minutes. Remove from heat. In a separate bowl, toss cucumbers, onion, pepper, mint and sesame seeds; add vinegar mixture. Marinate in refrigerator until ready to serve.

NEXT Preheat grill to medium-high heat. Combine ground chicken, teriyaki sauce, sesame oil, scallions, basil, cilantro and mint in a large bowl; season with salt and pepper. Divide mixture into 4 equal-size patties, about 1 inch thick.

LAST Oil grill grates and sear burgers 2 minutes per side; remove burgers from grill and lightly cover with aluminum foil. Lower the grill temperature to medium-low; place plank on grill and heat 3 minutes. Using tongs, turn plank over and place burgers directly on the heated side. Close lid and grill 15 minutes, or until a meat thermometer reaches 165°. Remove plank and burgers from grill. Top burgers with marinated salad and serve on toasted buns.

NOTE To cook the burgers without a plank, preheat a grill or grill pan to medium-high heat; cook for 6 minutes per side, or until the internal temperature reaches 165°.

ALDER-PLANKED TURKEY BURGERS WITH CHIPOTLE KETCHUP

Ground turkey doesn't usually have much flavor, but these burgers take on the smoky essence of the alder, and the smoked Gouda takes it to another level.

PLACE indoor/outdoor
PREP TIME soak + 15 minutes
COOK TIME 12 to 20 minutes
YIELD 4 servings

1½ pounds ground turkey
½ cup finely chopped green bell pepper
1 teaspoon chili powder
½ teaspoon ground cumin
¼ teaspoon red pepper flakes
½ teaspoon kosher salt
2 ounces smoked Gouda,
    cut into ¼-inch-square cubes
1 15-inch alder grilling plank, soaked
4 whole-wheat hamburger buns
sautéed onions

CHIPOTLE KETCHUP

1 cup ketchup
1 tablespoon lime juice
2 teaspoons chipotle peppers in
    adobo sauce, finely chopped
½ teaspoon ground cumin

FIRST Combine ingredients for ketchup in a small bowl; refrigerate until needed. Makes 1 cup.

NEXT Place ground turkey in a large bowl; add bell pepper, chili powder, cumin, red pepper, and salt. Gently fold spices into meat and add cheese. Divide into 4 equal-size patties, about 1 inch thick. (If too much cheese is visible, use your fingers to push it inside the patties so the cheese will melt inside the burger and not on the grill.)

LAST Preheat grill to high heat. Oil grill grates and sear burgers 3 minutes per side, until grill marks form. Remove burgers from grill; put on a plate and lightly cover with foil. Reduce grill temperature to medium-low and place soaked plank on grill. Heat 3 minutes, then turn plank over and put burgers on the heated side. Cook 18 to 20 minutes, or until internal temperature reaches 165°. Remove plank and burgers from grill. Place burgers on bun; top with chipotle ketchup and caramelized onions, if desired.

NOTE To cook the burgers without a plank, preheat a grill or grill pan to medium-high heat; cook for 6 minutes per side, or until the internal temperature reaches 165°.

PLANKED FISH TACOS WITH CORN SALSA AND GUACAMOLE

To make these tacos, use whatever fish is in season, and then get creative with the toppings. If you don't have time to make your own, purchase fresh salsa at your local market.

PLACE outdoor
PREP TIME soak + 5 minutes
COOK TIME 15 minutes
YIELD 4 servings

FISH

2 teaspoons chili powder
2 teaspoons ground cumin
2 teaspoons brown sugar
1½ pounds salmon, snapper, halibut or tuna fillets
1 15-inch cedar, maple or alder plank, soaked
8 8-inch flour tortillas, warmed

CORN AND MINT SALSA

2 cups frozen corn kernels, thawed
1 small red onion, diced
1 small jalapeño, minced
½ cup chopped mint leaves
2 tablespoons fresh lime juice
¾ cup chopped tomatoes

GUACAMOLE

2 ripe avocados, diced
½ medium red onion, diced
¼ cup fresh chopped cilantro
¼ cup fresh lime juice

FIRST Make the salsa by mixing the ingredients and seasoning with salt and pepper; set aside. For the guacamole, mash the avocado lightly with a fork. Add the onion, cilantro and lime juice; mix together.

NEXT Preheat grill to medium-low. In a small bowl, combine chili powder, cumin and sugar. Season fillets with salt and pepper, then rub on desired amount of spice mixture. Place soaked plank on grill; close lid and heat plank 3 minutes. Turn plank over; place fillets on heated side and close lid. Cook 12 minutes for medium, or until desired doneness.

LAST Remove fish and plank from grill; allow fillets to rest 3 minutes before serving. Flake fish and serve in tortillas with salsa and guacamole.

SHRIMP AND B.L.T. TACOS
WITH AVOCADO CRÈME

A classic combo makes its way to the tortilla. And this avocado crème can be used
on everything — as a sandwich spread or topping for grilled or planked fish.

PLACE indoor/outdoor
PREP TIME 10 minutes
COOK TIME 10 minutes
YIELD 4 servings

1 pound large shrimp, peeled and deveined
2 teaspoons olive oil
1 15-inch alder grilling plank, soaked
8 strips bacon, cooked
2 medium tomatoes, chopped
¼ head iceberg lettuce, thinly sliced
8 8-inch flour tortillas, warmed

AVOCADO CRÈME
1 avocado, diced
2 tablespoons fresh lime juice
¼ cup sour cream
¼ teaspoon ground cumin
1 to 3 tablespoons water,
    depending on desired consistency

FIRST To make avocado creme, Cut avocado into large chunks; place in blender or food processor. Add lime juice, sour cream and cumin; purée. Slowly add enough water to get a smooth consistency, scraping sides as necessary. Season with salt and cayenne pepper to taste. Set aside.

NEXT Preheat grill to medium-low heat. Season shrimp with salt and pepper; toss with oil. Place soaked plank on grill; close lid and heat 3 minutes. Turn plank over, using tongs; place shrimp on heated side. Close lid and cook 10 minutes, or until shrimp turn pink. Remove shrimp and plank from grill; tent with foil.

LAST Assemble tacos by spreading 1 tablespoon avocado crème onto each tortilla. Top with ⅛ portion of shrimp, one bacon strip, shredded lettuce and diced tomato.

NOTE Shrimp can also be prepared without planking, outdoors on a grill or indoors on a grill pan.

HUMMUS AND ARUGULA PIZZA

This recipe makes a perfect light meal and takes only minutes to prepare.
You can divide the pizzas into smaller servings to use as appetizers
or a side dish for tomato soup.

PLACE indoor
PREP TIME 10 minutes
COOK TIME 15 minutes
YIELD 4 main-course or 12 appetizer servings

PIZZA

1 14-ounce can refrigerated pizza dough
2 tablespoons olive oil
1 tablespoon lemon juice
1 teaspoon Dijon mustard
4 cups baby arugula
Parmesan curls, for garnish

HUMMUS

1 14½-ounce can chickpeas, rinsed and drained
½ cup chicken stock
¼ cup olive oil
2 teaspoons lemon zest
1 teaspoon ground cumin
1 clove garlic
Cayenne pepper

FIRST To make hummus, combine ingredients in a food processor, adding cayenne to taste; blend until smooth. Add more chicken stock, if necessary, so the mixture is smooth and easily spreadable; set aside.

NEXT Preheat oven to 400°. Roll out pizza dough and press onto a greased cookie sheet to form a 10x14-inch rectangle. Cut in half, horizontally, to form two 5x14-inch rectangles. Bake for 7 minutes, or until crusts start to brown; turn crusts over and continue cooking for another 5 minutes or until slightly brown.

LAST Spread ½ cup hummus onto each crust, leaving ½-inch borders along edges. In a large bowl, whisk oil, lemon juice and mustard. Add arugula and gently toss; season with salt and pepper. Top each pizza half with arugula mixture; garnish with Parmesan curls.

BBQ CHICKEN PIZZA

This pizza is especially good plank-grilled;
the resulting smoky flavor is a great match for the barbecue sauce.

PLACE indoor/outdoor
PREP TIME 15 minutes
COOK TIME 20 minutes
YIELD 4 to 6 servings

PIZZA

1 14-ounce can refrigerated pizza dough
⅓ cup red onion, thinly sliced
1 cup thinly sliced pineapple
1½ cup cooked, shredded
　　rotisserie chicken
2 cups smoked mozzarella, grated
2 15-inch cedar or maple grilling
　　planks, soaked

SAUCE

3 tablespoons olive oil
¼ cup tomato paste
3 tablespoons Worcestershire sauce
2 tablespoons brown sugar
2 tablespoons apple cider vinegar

FIRST In a small saucepan, combine the olive oil, tomato paste, Worcestershire sauce, brown sugar and apple cider vinegar. Heat over medium-low heat 5 minutes; set aside.

NEXT Preheat oven to 400°. Roll out pizza dough and press onto a greased cookie sheet to form a 10x14-inch rectangle. Cut in half, horizontally, to form two 5x14-inch rectangles. Bake for 7 minutes, or until crusts starts to brown; turn crusts over and continue cooking for another 5 minutes or until slightly brown.

LAST Preheat grill to medium-low heat. Spread barbecue sauce over each crust, leaving ½-inch borders along edges. Top pizzas with sliced onion, pineapple, shredded chicken and cheese. Finish in oven or on grill.

OVEN Continue baking pizza for another 7 minutes, or until cheese is bubbly and crust is golden brown.

GRILL Place planks on grill; close lid and heat 3 minutes. Turn planks over, using tongs; place pizzas on heated sides. Close lid; cook for 10 minutes, or until cheese is bubbly.

PROSCIUTTO, ASPARAGUS AND RICOTTA PIZZA

Pair this pizza with a simple salad for a delicious last-minute meal.

PLACE indoor/outdoor
PREP TIME 10 minutes
COOK TIME 12 minutes
YIELD 4 to 6 servings

1 14-ounce can refrigerated pizza dough
½ cup marinara sauce
1½ cups shredded mozzarella cheese
½ cup grated Parmesan cheese
6 very thin slices proscuitto
10 spears asparagus,
    blanched (see page 22)
½ cup ricotta cheese
2 cloves garlic, minced

FIRST Preheat oven to 400°. Roll out pizza dough and press onto a greased cookie sheet to form a 10x14-inch rectangle. Cut in half, horizontally, to form two 5x14-inch rectangles. Bake for 7 minutes, or until crusts start to brown; turn crusts over and continue baking for another 5 minutes or until slightly brown.

NEXT Spread ¼ cup marinara sauce onto each crust, leaving ½-inch border along edges. Top each pizza with ¾ cup mozzarella and ¼ cup Parmesan. Place prosciutto slices, in a single layer, across pizzas; arrange asparagus spears so they run perpendicular to the pizza, about 3 inches apart. Top with heaping teaspoons of ricotta and minced garlic.

LAST Finish in oven or on grill.

OVEN Continue baking pizza for another 7 minutes, or until cheese is bubbly and crust is golden brown.

GRILL Preheat grill to medium-low heat. Place planks on grill; close lid and heat 3 minutes. Turn planks over, using tongs; place pizzas on heated sides. Close lid; cook for 10 minutes, or until cheese is bubbly.

SPANISH SHRIMP PIZZA

Manchego, a classic Spanish cheese, is made from sheep's milk
and has a wonderful flavor. If you can't find it in your local market,
shredded mozzarella is a good substitute.

PLACE indoor/outdoor
PREP TIME 15 minutes
COOK TIME 20 minutes
YIELD 4 to 6 servings

PIZZA

1 14-ounce can refrigerated pizza dough
1 cup fresh spinach leaves
½ cup red onion, thinly sliced
7 ounces small cooked shrimp, peeled
1 cup shredded manchego cheese
2 ounces crumbled goat cheese
¼ cup kalamata olives, finely chopped
2 15-inch cedar planks

SAUCE

1 12-ounce jar roasted red peppers, drained
1 garlic clove, crushed
1 tablespoon olive oil
1 tablespoon balsamic vinegar
¼ cup fresh basil, chopped
Red pepper flakes

FIRST In a food processor or blender, combine sauce ingredients. Blend until smooth. Season with red pepper flakes and salt; set aside.

NEXT Preheat oven to 400°. Roll out pizza dough and press onto a greased cookie sheet to form a 10x14-inch rectangle. Cut in half, horizontally, to form two 5x14-inch rectangles. Bake for 7 minutes, or until crusts start to brown; turn crusts over and continue cooking for another 5 minutes or until slightly brown.

LAST Spread ¼ cup sauce over each crust, leaving ½-inch borders along edges. Top pizzas with spinach, onion, shrimp, manchego, goat cheese and olives. Finish in oven or on grill.

OVEN Continue baking pizza for another 7 minutes, or until cheese is bubbly and crust is golden brown.

GRILL Preheat grill to medium-low heat. Place planks on grill; close lid and heat 3 minutes. Turn planks over, using tongs; place pizzas on heated sides. Close lid; cook for 10 minutes, or until cheese is bubbly.

ROSEMARY WHITE BEAN SOUP

This classic white-bean soup is one of my favorites during the winter.
With layers of flavor, it makes a hearty meal with nothing more
than a simple green salad.

PLACE indoor
PREP TIME 10 minutes
COOK TIME 25 minutes
YIELD 8 servings

2 tablespoons olive oil
1 large onion, diced
5 cloves garlic, minced
4 cans great northern beans, drained and rinsed
4 cups chicken or vegetable stock
1 5-inch sprig of fresh rosemary
  (or 1 tablespoon dried)
½ cup sun-dried tomatoes chopped
  (not packed in oil)
Fresh Parmesan cheese, finely grated (optional)

FIRST Heat oil in a 5-quart pot over medium heat. Add onion; sauté for 3 minutes or until softened. Stir in garlic and continue cooking for an additional minute. Add beans, stock, rosemary and tomatoes. Season with salt and simmer for 20 minutes.

LAST Discard rosemary stem; season with salt and pepper to taste. Top each bowl of soup with Parmesan cheese and serve.

CHAPTER FOUR | Simple Gourmet

SEAFOOD

Fish takes on a whole different role and becomes delicious and easy to prepare at home.
The perfect complement to the smoky flavors of grilling, it can also be cooked
indoors or combined with the simplest ingredients for an impressive and unique dish.

CEDAR-WRAPPED HALIBUT
WITH FRESH VEGETABLE RELISH

Fish cooked in cedar papers is completely foolproof and makes a beautiful presentation.

PLACE indoor/outdoor
PREP TIME 10 minutes
COOK TIME 10 minutes
YIELD 4 servings

4 six- to eight-ounce halibut fillets
1 tablespoon olive oil
½ large red onion, diced
1 medium yellow bell pepper, chopped
2 small tomatoes, chopped
3 tablespoons white wine vinegar
1 tablespoon sugar
¼ cup chopped flat-leaf parsley
½ cup chopped green olives
2 tablespoons capers
1 tablespoon freshly grated lemon zest
4 ten-inch or 8 six-inch cedar papers, soaked

FIRST Season fish with salt and pepper; set aside while preparing relish. Heat oil in a large saucepan over medium heat; add onion and sauté until lightly softened, about 1 minute. Add bell pepper and tomatoes; continue to cook 2 to 3 more minutes. Add vinegar and sugar, cooking until they are incorporated, about 2 minutes. Remove pan from heat and add parsley, olives, capers and lemon zest. Season with salt and pepper; set aside.

NEXT Preheat grill or grill pan to medium heat. Place 1 halibut fillet in the center of each grilling paper, dividing the 4 fillets if you're using six-inch papers. Fold the edges of the papers over the fillets, securing with cotton string if necessary.

LAST Place packets seam side down on grill; cook 4 minutes, then turn and cook 4 minutes on the other side. To serve, open packets and spoon relish over fish.

PLANKED SALMON
WITH ASIAN BARBECUE SAUCE

Plank grilling gives salmon a moist, delicious flavor.
The sauce is just as easy to make but gives the dish an exotic touch —
and it's as good on chicken or pork as it is on salmon.

PLACE outdoor
PREP TIME soak + 5 minutes
COOK TIME 15 minutes
YIELD 4 servings

SALMON

4 six-ounce salmon fillets
  or a single 1½-pound fillet
1 15-inch cedar, maple
  or alder grilling plank, soaked
1 tablespoon sesame seeds

SAUCE

¼ cup ketchup
¼ cup hoisin sauce
2 tablespoons rice vinegar
1 tablespoon soy sauce
1 tablespoon toasted sesame oil
1 tablespoon grated fresh ginger
½ teaspoon crushed red pepper

FIRST Combine sauce ingredients in a medium bowl. Divide in half, using one-half for basting and reserving the other to serve with the salmon.

NEXT Preheat grill to medium-low heat. Brush half of the sauce on the salmon, then sprinkle with sesame seeds. Place soaked plank on the grill, close the lid and allow plank to heat 3 minutes. Turn plank over, place salmon directly on heated side and close the lid again. Cook 12 minutes (for medium), or until desired doneness.

LAST Remove salmon and plank from grill and allow to rest 3 minutes. Serve with the remaining barbecue sauce.

CEDAR-WRAPPED SALMON WITH BALSAMIC SAUCE

This is a simple but sophisticated dish.
The sauce is versatile, and it's delicious served over grilled pork.

PLACE indoor/outdoor
PREP TIME 10 minutes
COOK TIME 10 minutes
YIELD 4 servings

SALMON

4 six-ounce salmon fillets
1 teaspoon fresh thyme leaves
4 ten-inch or 8 six-inch cedar papers, soaked

BALSAMIC SAUCE

½ tablespoon butter
¼ cup balsamic vinegar
2 tablespoons brown sugar
½ tablespoon whole-grain mustard
1 large garlic clove, smashed

FIRST To make the sauce, melt butter over low heat; add remaining ingredients. Cook over medium low heat until reduced and thick, about 4 to 5 minutes. Remove garlic clove and set aside.

NEXT Preheat grill or grill pan to medium heat. Season salmon with salt and pepper. Place one fillet in the center of each grilling paper, dividing the four fillets if you're using six-inch papers. Fold the edges of the papers over the fillets, securing with cotton string if necessary. Place packets seam side down on grill; cook 5 to 6 minutes depending on thickness of fish.

LAST Remove packets from grill, using tongs. Open and serve salmon immediately with Balsamic Sauce.

PLANKED MOROCCAN SALMON

This Moroccan rub can be used on seafood, chicken, pork—even sweet potatoes. Double the recipe and keep some in the pantry for a head start on a quick weeknight dinner.

PLACE outdoor
PREP TIME soak + 5 minutes
COOK TIME 15 minutes
YIELD 4 servings

SALMON
4 six-ounce salmon fillets or
   one 1½-pound salmon fillet
1 15-inch cedar or alder
   grilling plank, soaked

RUB
1 teaspoon brown sugar
½ teaspoon curry powder
½ teaspoon coriander
½ teaspoon cumin
½ teaspoon paprika
½ teaspoon cinnamon
½ teaspoon kosher salt
½ teaspoon black pepper
2 teaspoons olive oil

FIRST Preheat grill to medium-low heat. To make rub, combine all ingredients except olive oil in a small bowl; set aside. Brush salmon fillets with olive oil then rub with spice blend, coating top and sides of each fillet.

NEXT Place soaked plank on grill; close lid and heat 3 minutes. Turn plank over; place salmon directly on heated side and close lid. Cook salmon 12 minutes (for medium), or until desired doneness.

LAST Remove salmon and plank from grill; allow fillets to rest 3 minutes before serving.

MAPLE-PLANKED SNAPPER WITH ARTICHOKE PESTO

The lemony garlic flavor of this pesto adds a bright flavor to any fish. Try it on halibut, mahi-mahi, or cod. It's also great on grilled chicken breasts or tossed with pasta.

PLACE indoor/outdoor
PREP TIME soak + 10 minutes
COOK TIME 15 minutes
YIELD 4 servings

FISH
1 15-inch maple grilling plank, soaked
4 six- to eight-ounce snapper fillets
1 tablespoon olive oil

PESTO
1 14-ounce can artichoke hearts, drained
1 cup fresh parsley leaves
½ cup toasted walnuts, chopped
2 large cloves garlic, peeled
1 lemon, zested and juiced
½ cup reduced-sodium chicken broth
2 tablespoons olive oil
⅓ cup grated Pecorino Romano or Parmesan

FIRST In a food processor, combine artichoke hearts, parsley, walnuts, garlic, lemon juice and zest, chicken broth and olive oil. Blend until smooth, adding more olive oil if necessary; pesto should be thick and slightly creamy. Transfer pesto to bowl; stir in cheese. Season with salt and pepper and set aside until ready to serve.

NEXT Prepare fish on grill or in oven.

GRILL Preheat grill to medium-low heat. Season fish fillets with salt and pepper. Place soaked plank on grill; close lid and heat 3 minutes. Turn plank over and place fish directly on heated side. Drizzle fish with olive oil and close lid. Cook 12 minutes, or until desired doneness. Remove fish and plank from grill. Allow to rest 3 minutes before serving.

OVEN Preheat oven to 375°. Place fish fillets in an oven-safe dish coated with cooking spray. Drizzle fish with olive oil; season with salt and pepper. Bake 20 minutes, or until fish flakes easily with a fork.

LAST Transfer fish to serving platter. Top each fillet with 2 tablespoons of pesto.

CEDAR-WRAPPED SHRIMP
WITH ASIAN TOMATO SALSA

The unique flavor of this salsa sets it apart from more traditional versions.
Serve with crispy won tons for an easy appetizer.

PLACE indoor/outdoor
PREP TIME 15 minutes
COOK TIME 8 minutes
YIELD 4 servings

SHRIMP

1½ pounds large shrimp, peeled and
  deveined, tails intact
4 ten-inch or 8 six-inch cedar papers, soaked

SALSA

2 medium tomatoes, chopped
½ English cucumber, diced
2 scallions, sliced
¼ cup chopped fresh mint
1 small jalapeño, finely chopped
2 tablespoons rice vinegar
2 teaspoons soy sauce
1 teaspoon toasted sesame oil
1 tablespoon sesame seeds

FIRST To prepare salsa, combine all ingredients in a medium bowl. Season with salt and pepper; set aside.

LAST Preheat grill or grill pan to medium heat. Season shrimp with salt and pepper, then divide equally among soaked papers. Fold the edges of the papers over the shrimp, securing with cotton string if necessary. Place shrimp packets on grill; cook 3 minutes per side, or until shrimp are pink. Remove from grill and serve immediately with Asian salsa.

PLANKED SHRIMP
WITH LIME CILANTRO BUTTER

Although I don't cook with too much butter, this one is packed
so full of flavor that all you need is a little. Keep some in your freezer
to top grilled fish or chicken anytime.

PLACE indoor/outdoor
PREP TIME soak + 10 minutes
COOK TIME 10 minutes
YIELD 4 servings

SHRIMP
1½ pounds large shrimp, peeled, tails intact
1 15-inch alder, maple or oak grilling plank

BUTTER
4 tablespoons unsalted butter, softened
½ lime, zested and juiced
1 teaspoon cilantro, finely chopped

FIRST In a bowl, combine softened butter and lime juice; stir until juice is incorporated. Stir in zest, cilantro, and salt and pepper to taste. Store in refrigerator until ready to use.

NEXT Prepare shrimp on grill or grill pan.

OUTDOOR Preheat grill to medium-low heat. Place plank on grill; close lid and heat 3 minutes. Turn plank over and place shrimp directly on heated side. Close grill lid and cook 10 minutes, or until shrimp are firm and pink.

INDOOR Preheat grill pan over medium-high heat. Coat pan with cooking spray or olive oil. Grill shrimp 2 minutes per side, or until they are firm and pink.

LAST Toss shrimp with 2 to 3 tablespoons of cilantro butter, just enough to coat. Serve immediately.

TERIYAKI TUNA WITH SWEET AND SOUR CUCUMBERS

If you prefer your tuna rare, prepare it indoors in a grill pan;
it only takes a couple of minutes to cook. And this traditional teriyaki sauce
is so easy you'll never want anything but homemade again.

PLACE indoor/outdoor
PREP TIME 20 minutes + marinate
COOK TIME 5 minutes
YIELD 4 servings

TUNA

½ cup sugar

2 tablespoons water

1 teaspoon lemon juice

½ cup soy sauce

3 slices fresh ginger, the size of a quarter

1 clove garlic, sliced

1 tablespoon vegetable oil

1 pound tuna steak

SWEET AND SPICY CUCUMBERS

⅓ cup rice vinegar

1 teaspoon sugar

2 teaspoons soy sauce

1 teaspoon sesame oil

1 small red chili pepper, thinly sliced
   (or ½ teaspoon chili paste)

1½ cups thinly sliced English cucumbers

FIRST To make Sweet and Spicy Cucumbers, combine vinegar, sugar, soy sauce and sesame oil into a medium bowl; stir until sugar dissolves. Add chili pepper and cucumbers to vinegar mixture and set aside 20 minutes, to develop flavors.

NEXT In a small saucepan, combine sugar, water and lemon juice. Simmer, stirring occasionally, until the mixture begins to turn golden brown, about 5 to 7 minutes. Remove pan from heat and slowly add soy sauce. Stir until sugar is dissolved. Stir in ginger and garlic. Set aside and let cool 15 minutes. Then, place tuna in zip-top plastic bag. Strain teriyaki sauce, then pour half of the liquid over the tuna, saving the other half to use for dipping. Seal bag, pressing out as much air as possible. Refrigerate tuna; let marinate at least 15 minutes.

LAST Preheat grill or grill pan to high heat. Brush grill grates with oil, then remove tuna from marinade. Sear tuna 1 minute per side (for rare), or until desired doneness. Slice tuna against the grain and arrange on plates. Garnish with Sweet and Spicy Cucumbers and serve with remaining teriyaki sauce for dipping.

SCALLOPS WITH GRILLED PINEAPPLE SALSA

This colorful dish makes a beautiful presentation.
If you're short on time, you don't have to grill the pineapple,
but it does add a nice depth of flavor.

PLACE indoor/outdoor
PREP TIME 15 minutes
COOK TIME 15 minutes
YIELD 4 servings

SCALLOPS
16 large sea scallops (about 1¼ pounds)
1 tablespoon olive oil
1 tablespoon lime zest

SALSA
1 medium pineapple, trimmed and
    cored into 8 slices, ½-inch thick
1 small red onion, finely diced
1 green jalapeño, finely diced
2 limes, juiced
2 tablespoons chopped cilantro
2 tablespoons chopped mint
½ teaspoon salt

FIRST Preheat grill to high heat. Brush grill grates with vegetable oil, then grill pineapple slices 4 minutes per side, or until grill marks form. Remove pineapple from grill; cut into ½-inch sections and place in a medium bowl. Add remaining salsa ingredients; combine well and set aside.

NEXT Blot scallops dry with paper towels; drizzle with olive oil, coating scallops on all sides. Season with lime zest, salt and black pepper.

LAST Brush grill grates with vegetable oil. Grill scallops 2 to 3 minutes per side, until just opaque in the center. Serve with pineapple salsa.

PLANKED PROSCIUTTO-WRAPPED SWORDFISH SKEWERS

Because it has a steak-like texture, swordfish is an excellent choice for grilling. These skewers, served in smaller portions, also make impressive appetizers.

PLACE indoor/outdoor
PREP TIME 15 minutes
COOK TIME 10 minutes
YIELD 4 servings

1½ pounds swordfish fillets,
    cut into 1½-inch cubes
1 tablespoon olive oil
1 tablespoon fresh rosemary, chopped
10 thin slices prosciutto,
    cut into 1-inch-long strips
8 12-inch metal or wooden skewers
2 maple or alder grilling planks, soaked
4 lemon wedges

FIRST If using wooden skewers, soak in water 15 minutes. In a large bowl, toss swordfish cubes with 1 tablespoon of oil and rosemary; season with pepper. Wrap a prosciutto strip around each fish cube and skewer, securing the prosciutto around the fish. Divide cubes among the 4 skewers.

NEXT Preheat grill to medium-low heat. Place planks on grill; close lid and heat 3 minutes. Turn planks over and place skewers directly on heated sides. Close lid and cook 10 to 12 minutes, or until fish is cooked through.

LAST Remove plank and fish skewers from grill. Serve immediately with lemon wedges.

NOTE To prepare these skewers directly on an indoor or outdoor grill, oil grill grates and grill fish over medium-high heat for 1 to 1½ minutes on all four sides.

POULTRY

Whether roasted, plank grilled or sautéed with the freshest ingredients, basic chicken can easily be turned into something fabulous with very little effort.

MEDITERRANEAN
STUFFED CHICKEN BREASTS

This recipe doesn't have to be planked, but it's well worth the extra few minutes.
Perfect for entertaining, your guests will never know how easy it is
to create this gourmet dish.

PLACE indoor/outdoor
PREP TIME 15 minutes
COOK TIME 25 minutes
YIELD 4 servings

3 teaspoons olive oil, divided
⅓ cup chopped shallots
1½ teaspoons sugar
4 small garlic cloves, minced
1½ tablespoons balsamic vinegar
½ cup goat cheese
½ cup sun-dried tomatoes,
    rehydrated in hot water
¼ cup chopped fresh basil
½ teaspoon chopped fresh rosemary
    (or ¼ teaspoon dried)
4 boneless, skinless chicken breasts
1 15-inch alder or maple grilling
    plank, soaked

FIRST Heat 1 teaspoon olive oil in pan; sauté shallots, sugar and garlic until softened, about 3 minutes. Remove mixture from pan; place in a medium bowl and stir in vinegar. Add cheese, tomatoes, basil and rosemary. Mix well.

NEXT Make a horizontal cut in the side of each chicken breast to form a pocket. Stuff each pocket with 2 rounded tablespoons of the mixture. Coat chicken breasts with the remaining oil; salt and pepper to taste.

LAST Cook chicken breasts, indoors or out.

OUTDOORS Preheat grill to medium-low heat. Place soaked plank on grill and close lid. Heat the plank for 3 minutes then turn it over; place chicken on heated side of the plank. Close grill lid again and cook 20 minutes, or until the chicken is no longer pink in center or a meat thermometer registers 165°.

INDOORS Sear chicken breasts for 2 minutes on each side over medium-high heat. Bake in a 350° oven for 20 minutes, or until a meat thermometer registers 165°.

HERB CHICKEN PAILLARDS
WITH ARTICHOKE-TOMATO SALSA

This salsa is a perfect match to these quick-cooking chicken breasts.
I also use it on everything from pasta to grilled fish.

PLACE indoor/outdoor
PREP TIME 15 minutes
COOK TIME 8 minutes
YIELD 4 servings

CHICKEN

4 six- to eight-ounce boneless,
    skinless chicken breast cutlets

2 tablespoons olive oil

1 lemon, halved and juiced

2 teaspoons oregano

1 clove garlic, peeled and slightly smashed

SALSA

1 cup chopped fresh tomatoes

⅓ cup quartered artichoke hearts

¼ cup chopped kalamata olives

2 tablespoons chopped fresh basil

1 garlic clove, minced

1 tablespoon chopped Italian parsley

1 tablespoon red wine vinegar

1 teaspoon olive oil

FIRST Combine salsa ingredients in a medium bowl; season with salt and pepper. Salsa can be made up to one day in advance, but bring to room temperature before serving.

NEXT Preheat grill or grill pan to high heat. Place chicken cutlets in a large zip-top plastic bag. Add olive oil, lemon juice, oregano, garlic, salt and pepper. Turn to coat chicken; marinate in the refrigerator 15 minutes.

LAST Oil grill grates or pan. Grill cutlets 2 to 3 minutes per side, or until lightly browned and cooked through. Remove chicken from grill and serve with salsa.

INDIAN CHICKEN KABOBS

This dish is packed full of exotic flavors but is deceptively simple to make.

PLACE indoor/outdoor
PREP TIME 15 minutes
COOK TIME 8 minutes
YIELD 4 servings

2 limes, halved and juiced
3 tablespoons olive oil
2 cloves garlic, peeled and lightly smashed
1 tablespoon curry powder
2 teaspoons cumin
2 teaspoons ground ginger
1 teaspoon cinnamon
2 pounds boneless, skinless chicken breasts,
    cut into 1½-inch cubes
8 wooden skewers
Chopped cilantro for garnish
4 lime wedges
1 cup store-purchased mango chutney

FIRST Soak wooden skewers in water 15 minutes. In a large zip-top bag, combine lime juice, olive oil, garlic, curry powder, cumin, ginger and cinnamon. Add chicken to the bag and toss to coat; marinate in the refrigerator 15 minutes.

NEXT Preheat grill or grill pan to medium-high heat. Thread 4 to 5 pieces of chicken on each skewer; season with salt and pepper. Oil grill grates, then cook kabobs until brown on one side, about 3 minutes. Keep moving the kabobs a quarter of a turn until all sides are brown and meat is opaque at the edges, about 2 minutes per side. Cut into a piece of chicken to make sure no pink is visible before removing it from the grill.

LAST Transfer kabobs to a large platter and top with chopped cilantro. Serve with lime wedges and mango chutney.

BRINED AND GRILLED ORANGE TARRAGON CHICKEN

Brining is a simple technique and results in tender, juicy chicken.
This concentrated version takes only 25 minutes instead of the traditional 6 hours.

PLACE indoor/outdoor
PREP TIME brine + 10 minutes
COOK TIME 25 minutes
YIELD 4 servings

BRINE
½ cup kosher salt
½ cup sugar
2 cups hot water
2 cups cold water
4 bone-in skinless chicken breasts

WET RUB
½ cup orange marmalade
¼ cup whole-grain Dijon mustard
2 tablespoons cider vinegar
2 tablespoons tarragon, coarsely chopped

FIRST In a large bowl, combine salt, sugar and hot water; stir until dissolved. Add cold water and chicken. Refrigerate 25 minutes but no longer.

NEXT In another bowl, combine marmalade, mustard, cider vinegar and tarragon. Divide marmalade mixture in half and set aside.

LAST Preheat grill to medium-high heat. Remove chicken from brine, pat dry and sprinkle with pepper. Brush grill grates with olive oil and place chicken, meat side down, on grill. Cook until well browned, about 5 minutes per side. Move chicken to cooler side of grill. Brush liberally with half of marmalade mixture; continue cooking 10 minutes, or until internal temperature reaches 165°.

NOTE To cook indoors, preheat oven to 450°. Place chicken in oven-safe dish coated with cooking spray. Bake 20 minutes. Brush with half of marmalade mixture and return to oven for an additional 15 minutes, or until internal temperature reaches 165°.

MAPLE-PLANKED APRICOT CHICKEN

When in season, I like to substitute the apricots in this dish with fresh peaches and peach preserves.

PLACE indoor/outdoor
PREP TIME soak + 10 minutes
COOK TIME 30 minutes
YIELD 4 servings

2 slices whole-wheat sandwich bread
¼ cup apricot preserves
2 teaspoons soy sauce
2 teaspoons grated ginger
2 teaspoons balsamic vinegar
1 clove garlic, chopped
¼ teaspoon red pepper flakes
4 fresh apricots, halved and pitted
4 six-ounce boneless, skinless chicken breasts
1 tablespoon olive oil
1 maple grilling plank, soaked

FIRST Preheat grill to medium-low heat. Coarsely chop bread in a blender or food processor and set aside. In a small bowl, combine preserves, soy sauce, ginger, vinegar, garlic and red pepper flakes. Toss apricot halves with 1 tablespoon of preserves mixture and set aside.

NEXT Season chicken breasts generously with salt and pepper. Brush both sides of breasts with remaining apricot mixture, coating top side a little more generously. Top each breast with ¼ cup of the bread crumbs and drizzle with olive oil.

LAST Place soaked plank on grill; close lid and allow to heat 3 minutes. Turn plank over and place chicken breasts directly on heated side; close lid. Cook 25 minutes, or until internal temperature reaches 165°. Remove chicken and plank from grill. Loosely tent with foil and allow to rest 5 minutes before serving.

NOTE To make this dish indoors, preheat oven to 350°. Place bread-crumb-topped chicken in a 13x9-inch baking dish coated with cooking spray; bake 20 minutes, or until internal temperature reaches 165°.

GRILLED CHICKEN MOLE

If you prefer not to use a whole chicken, this dish can
easily be done with bone-in chicken breasts.
And the marinade really makes it something special.

PLACE outdoor
PREP TIME 10 minutes + marinate
COOK TIME 35 minutes
YIELD 4 servings

1 3½- to 4-pound chicken

MARINADE
½ cup soy sauce
4 tablespoons chipotle peppers
   in adobo sauce, finely chopped
2 tablespoons brown sugar
2 tablespoons cocoa powder
2 tablespoons vegetable oil
2 tablespoons fresh lime juice
1 tablespoon chopped garlic
2 teaspoons dried oregano
1 teaspoon freshly ground black pepper
½ teaspoon cinnamon

FIRST Using a sharp knife or poultry scissors, cut along both sides of the chicken's backbone and remove the bone. Place chicken breast-side-up on a cutting board, then flatten it by placing the heel of your hand over the breast-bone and pressing down firmly.

NEXT Put the chicken in a large zip-top bag. Combine all marinade ingredients in a medium bowl; add marinade to zip-top bag. Seal the bag, pressing out as much air as possible. Refrigerate 1 hour, turning chicken once.

LAST Preheat grill to medium heat. Place chicken skin side down on grill, close lid and cook 15 minutes, or until the chicken is nicely browned. Turn chicken over and continue cooking for 20 more minutes, or until an instant-read thermometer inserted into the thickest part of the thigh registers 170°. Transfer chicken to cutting board; let rest 10 minutes. Carve and serve.

MEAT

There is nothing better than filling your home with the wonderful aroma of well-prepared meats, and these simple recipes will help you do just that. Enjoy roasted lamb chops or a perfectly grilled steak, and welcome your friends and family.

PINEAPPLE AND RED PEPPER PORK SKEWERS WITH PEANUT SAUCE

These skewers plate beautifully and are perfect for a casual Saturday-night meal. Chicken, beef, or even salmon can easily be substituted for the pork.

PLACE indoor/outdoor
PREP TIME 15 minutes
COOK TIME 10 minutes
YIELD 4 servings

SKEWERS

1- to 1½-pound pork tenderloin, silver skin trimmed and cut into 1½-inch pieces

1 tablespoon soy sauce

1 tablespoon honey

1 medium red bell pepper, cut into 1½-inch pieces

9 ounces pineapple, cubed (1½ cups)

4 to 6 12-inch metal or wooden skewers

SAUCE

½ cup smooth peanut butter

½ cup chicken stock or water

1 tablespoon brown sugar

2 tablespoons soy sauce

2 tablespoons lime juice

¼ teaspoon crushed red pepper

FIRST To prepare the peanut sauce, combine ingredients in a small bowl and whisk with fork until smooth; set aside. (If using all-natural peanut butter, adjust the consistency by using more or less stock or water.)

NEXT Preheat grill or grill pan to medium-high heat. Toss pork cubes with soy and honey; season with salt and pepper. Alternately thread pork, pepper and pineapple onto skewers. (If using wooden skewers, soak in water for 15 minutes before using.)

LAST Oil the grate of your grill, then sear the skewers 2 minutes on all four sides, or until pork reaches an internal temperature of 145°.

APPLE GINGER STUFFED PORK CHOPS

You can save time by simply grilling a pork tenderloin and
using the stuffing as a delicious topping.

PLACE indoor/outdoor
PREP TIME soak + 15 minutes
COOK TIME 20 minutes
YIELD 4 servings

PORK

6 tablespoons whole-grain mustard
2 tablespoons balsamic vinegar
Salt and pepper
4 1½- to 2-inch-thick pork chops, bone-in
2 15-inch maple grilling planks, soaked

APPLE STUFFING

1 tablespoon butter
1 tablespoon olive oil
2 large apples,
     peeled and diced into ½-inch cubes
¼ cup chopped onions
1½ teaspoons grated ginger
½ cup dried cherries
½ cup chopped pecans
Salt and pepper

FIRST To make the stuffing, heat the butter and oil in a large skillet over medium heat. Add apples, onion and ginger; sauté 5 to 7 minutes, until the onions are tender and the apples are golden. Stir in dried cherries and chopped pecans; season with salt and pepper to taste.

NEXT Preheat grill or grill pan to medium-high heat. Using a sharp knife, slice horizontally into sides of the pork chops, almost to the bone, creating pockets for the stuffing. Stuff chops with apple mixture. In a small bowl, combine mustard and vinegar; season with salt and pepper. Coat each side of pork chops with ½ tablespoon of mustard mixture.

LAST Oil grill grates and place chops on grill; sear 2 minutes per side. Remove pork from grill and tent with foil. Reduce grill temperature to medium-low heat. Place planks on grill and close lid; heat 3 minutes. Using tongs, turn planks over and place pork directly on heated sides. Close lid; cook 20 minutes, or until internal temperature reaches 145°. Remove planks and chops from grill; let meat rest 5 minutes before serving.

NOTE To grill chops without planking, cook over medium-high heat for 6 minutes per side, or until internal temperature reaches 145°.

GRILLED PORK TENDERLOIN WITH SWEET ONION SAUCE

This recipe is easy enough to prepare on a weeknight but elegant enough for a dinner party.

PLACE indoor/outdoor
PREP TIME 10 minutes
COOK TIME 15 minutes
YIELD 4 servings

PORK

2 small pork tenderloins,
  about 20 ounces total, well trimmed
1 teaspoon salt
1 teaspoon black pepper

SAUCE

1 tablespoon olive oil
2 cloves garlic, minced
1 large onion, halved and thinly sliced
¼ cup balsamic vinegar
2 tablespoons brown sugar
1½ tablespoons tomato paste
½ teaspoon Chinese five-spice powder

FIRST To prepare the sauce, heat oil in a large skillet; add garlic and onion. Sauté until onions are well brown, about 5 minutes. Add vinegar, brown sugar, tomato paste and five-spice powder; continue cooking 1 minute, or until sauce slightly thickens. Remove skillet from heat and set aside. (This sauce is easy to reheat once you're ready to serve.)

LAST Preheat grill to medium-high heat. Season pork with salt and pepper. Oil grill grates; cook pork until browned on all four sides and internal temperature reaches 145°, about 2 to 3 minutes per side. Remove pork from grill and tent loosely with foil; allow meat to rest 5 minutes before serving. Slice pork and serve with sweet onion sauce.

BOURBON FLANK STEAK
WITH MANGO GINGER SALSA

This makes a great midweek meal. Put the steak and marinade in a zip-top bag, then throw it in the refrigerator before heading to work. When you get home, the meat is ready to grill.

PLACE indoor/outdoor
PREP TIME 15 minutes + marinate
COOK TIME 12 minutes
YIELD 4 servings

1½ pounds flank steak

MARINADE
¼ cup soy sauce
¼ cup bourbon
2 tablespoons brown sugar
2 teaspoons grated fresh ginger
2 teaspoons sesame oil
½ teaspoon red pepper flakes
2 cloves garlic, minced

SALSA
1 cup diced mango
⅓ cup diced tomatoes
3 tablespoons thinly sliced green onions
½ teaspoon chipotle peppers in
    adobo sauce, diced
½ teaspoon grated fresh ginger
1 tablespoon fresh lime juice

FIRST Combine marinade ingredients in a large zip-top bag; add flank steak, seal bag and turn to coat. Place in refrigerator and marinate 2 to 8 hours.

NEXT To prepare salsa, combine ingredients in a small bowl; set aside. Salsa can be prepared up to one day ahead; bring to room temperature before serving.

LAST Preheat grill to high heat. Place flank steak on grates; close lid and grill 6 minutes. Turn steak, grilling on the other side an additional 5 minutes. Using paring knife, cut a small slit in the thickest part of the meat to check for doneness. Meat should be rare, but if it requires a longer cooking time, place back on the grill with the thinner end of the steak over indirect heat. Continue cooking 1 to 2 minutes. (Steak should be slightly less done than preferred; it will continue to cook once it's removed from the grill.) Transfer meat to cutting board; cover loosely with foil and let rest 5 to 10 minutes. Slice thinly, on the bias against the grain.

NOTE To cook indoors, put flank steak in grill pan and cook over medium-high heat 3 to 4 minutes per side. Transfer to a 450° oven and roast about 5 minutes.

COFFEE-RUBBED BEEF FILETS

Beef is delicious cooked on an oak plank, but if you're short on time, simply grill it.
Surprisingly, coffee pairs beautifully with beef; for another layer of flavor,
top with crumbled blue cheese.

PLACE outdoor
PREP TIME soak + 5 minutes
COOK TIME 12 minutes
YIELD 4 servings

FILETS
4 six- to eight-ounce filet mignon or
    petite sirloin filets, ½-inch thick
1 15-inch oak grilling plank, soaked

RUB
2 tablespoons ground coffee
2 teaspoons brown sugar
1 teaspoon ancho chili powder
1 teaspoon allspice
1 teaspoon kosher salt
¼ teaspoon ground cinnamon

FIRST Preheat grill to high heat. In a small bowl, combine rub ingredients. Brush filets lightly with olive oil; apply coffee rub to filets, coating all sides.

NEXT Oil grill grates and sear filets, 1 minute per side. Remove steaks from grill and tent with aluminum foil.

LAST Reduce grill temperature to medium-low. Place soaked plank on grill; close lid and heat 3 minutes. Using tongs, turn plank over and place steaks directly on heated side. Close lid; cook 12 minutes (for medium), or until desired doneness. Remove plank and filets from grill; let meat rest 5 minutes before serving.

TUSCAN MARINATED NEW YORK STRIP

This simple marinade is delicious and works with any cut of beef.

PLACE outdoor
PREP TIME 10 minutes + marinate
COOK TIME 15 minutes
YIELD 4 servings

¼ cup vegetable oil
¼ cup red wine vinegar
2 tablespoons Dijon mustard
2 tablespoons fresh rosemary, chopped
2 teaspoons freshly ground black pepper
1 teaspoon salt
2 one-pound strip steaks, about 1¼ inches thick

FIRST Combine olive oil, vinegar, mustard, rosemary, salt and pepper in a large zip-top bag. Add steaks and toss to coat; marinate at room temperature 30 minutes, turning once.

NEXT Create two-level fire on a gas or charcoal grill, heating one side to high heat and the other to medium heat.

LAST Grill steaks on high 2 to 3 minutes per side, or until browned. Transfer to cooler side of grill; continue cooking about 5 minutes for rare (internal temperature of 125°) and 6 to 7 minutes for medium rare (internal temperature of 130°). Remove steaks from grill; loosely tent with foil and let rest 5 minutes before serving.

HERB-CRUSTED LAMB CHOPS WITH FETA TOPPING

Lemon and mint are perfect complements to lamb, making this dish unique and satisfying regardless of what taste you are in the mood for.

PLACE indoor/outdoor
PREP TIME 15 minutes
COOK TIME 20 minutes
YIELD 4 servings

½ cup chopped flat-leaf parsley
1 tablespoon fresh chopped rosemary leaves
1 large garlic clove, minced
Grated zest of 2 lemons
3 tablespoons olive oil
8 lamb loin or rib chops, each 1¼ inches thick
3 ounces feta cheese, crumbled
⅓ cup panko bread crumbs
1 15-inch cedar or oak grilling plank, soaked

FIRST Preheat grill to medium-low heat. In a small bowl, combine parsley, rosemary, garlic, lemon zest and olive oil. Season generously with salt and pepper. Combine half the mixture with bread crumbs and feta cheese; set aside. Rub remaining herb mixture on lamb chops before grilling.

LAST Place soaked plank on grill; close lid and heat 3 minutes. Using tongs, turn plank over and place lamb chops directly on heated side. Close lid; cook 6 minutes. Pat equal amounts of feta topping onto each chop. Close lid again and continue cooking 5 to 6 more minutes (for medium), or until desired doneness. (Meat thermometer should register 130°.) Remove chops and plank from grill; tent chops with aluminum foil and let rest 5 minutes before serving.

NOTE To cook indoors, sear chops in a large, ovenproof skillet over moderately high heat until browned on one side, about 3 minutes. Turn the chops over; top with equal amount of feta topping. Transfer to a 425° oven. Roast 5 to 8 minutes, or until desired doneness.

CHAPTER FIVE | Sides

MAPLE-PLANKED GREEN BEANS WITH BLUE CHEESE

I am always amazed at the rave reviews this dish receives. The extra layer of flavor provided by the planking makes something as simple as green beans special.

PLACE outdoor
PREP TIME soak + 15 minutes
COOK TIME 10 minutes
YIELD 4 servings

1 pound fresh, whole green beans, trimmed
1 tablespoon olive oil
½ cup pecan halves, toasted
3 ounces blue cheese, crumbled
1 15-inch maple or alder grilling plank, soaked

FIRST Preheat grill to medium-low heat. Cook green beans in a large pot of boiling water (seasoned with salt) until crisp, about 4 minutes. Remove beans from water; drain well and rinse with cold water to stop the cooking process.

NEXT Combine beans and olive oil in a large bowl; season with salt and pepper. Place soaked plank on grill; close lid and heat 3 minutes. Using tongs, turn plank over. Spread beans directly on heated side or in a grill basket set on top of heated plank; cook 10 to 12 minutes, or until beans are tender and edges begin to brown.

LAST Remove the beans and plank from grill. Place the beans in a large bowl and toss with blue cheese, pecans and freshly ground pepper. Serve immediately.

SAUTÉED BROCCOLI WITH ROASTED PEPPERS AND GOAT CHEESE

Once you try this dish, boring steamed broccoli will be a thing of the past.
You can change it up, too, by substituting feta or Parmesan for the goat cheese.

PLACE indoor
PREP TIME 10 minutes
COOK TIME 12 minutes
YIELD 4 servings

1 tablespoon olive oil
2 cloves garlic, minced
4 cups broccoli florets
3 tablespoons water
1 cup jarred roasted red peppers, cut into thin strips
1 teaspoon dried thyme
2 ounces goat cheese, crumbled

FIRST In a large skillet over medium heat, sauté garlic in oil until fragrant. Add broccoli and water; cook until broccoli is crisp tender, about 10 minutes. Stir in roasted peppers and thyme; season with salt and pepper.

LAST Top broccoli with crumbled goat cheese just before serving.

GRILLED VEGETABLES

The perfect accompaniment to any grilled or roasted meat,
grilled vegetables take only minutes to prepare. The beauty of this dish
is that you can use any type of vegetable, from asparagus to onions.

PLACE indoor/outdoor
PREP TIME 10 minutes
COOK TIME 8 minutes
YIELD 4 servings

VEGETABLES

2 large or 3 small zucchini

2 large or 3 small squash

2 Japanese eggplants

MARINADE

3 tablespoons shallots, chopped

⅓ cup white balsamic vinegar

¼ cup olive oil

1 tablespoon molasses

2 teaspoons dried oregano

2 teaspoons dried thyme

FIRST Cut off tips of squash, zucchini and eggplant; slice in half lengthwise and set aside. In a small bowl, combine marinade ingredients and pour into a large zip-top bag. Add vegetables; toss to coat. Marinate at room temperature 20 minutes, turning once.

LAST Preheat indoor grill pan or outdoor grill to medium-high heat. Oil grill grates. Place vegetables, skin side down, on grill; reserve marinade for later use. Cook 4 minutes per side until vegetables are tender. Remove from grill and drizzle with remaining marinade before serving.

PEANUT GINGER SOBA NOODLES

This makes the perfect side dish for almost any Asian entrée.
For a little extra color, add a few steamed snow peas.

PLACE indoor
PREP TIME 5 minutes
COOK TIME 10 minutes
YIELD 4 servings

SAUCE
2 tablespoons peanut butter
2 tablespoons soy sauce
1 tablespoon water
1 tablespoon honey
1 teaspoon sesame oil
1 teaspoon fresh grated ginger

5 ounces soba noodles or spaghetti
1 tablespoon sesame seeds
1½ tablespoons green onion, finely chopped

FIRST In a small bowl combine sauce ingredients and set aside.

NEXT In a large pot of boiling, salted water, add noodles; cook according to package directions. Drain and place pasta in a large bowl.

LAST While noodles are still hot, pour sauce over; season with salt and pepper. Gently toss, making sure peanut sauce covers noodles. Place in serving bowl or divide evenly among four plates. Garnish with sesame seeds and green onions.

SWEET POTATO FRITES

These potatoes are highly addictive. For a different twist,
use lime zest instead of orange and top them with some fresh cilantro.

PLACE indoor
PREP TIME 10 minutes
COOK TIME 30 minutes
YIELD 6 servings

FRITES

1½ pounds sweet potatoes
   (about 3 large potatoes)
1 tablespoon olive oil
1½ teaspoons ancho chili powder
1½ teaspoons paprika
1½ teaspoons kosher salt
3 teaspoons fresh grated orange zest

CHIPOTLE AIOLI

1 cup mayonnaise
2 tablespoons fresh lime juice
2 tablespoons brown sugar
1 tablespoon chipotle peppers
   in adobo sauce, finely chopped
1 teaspoon ground cumin

FIRST Combine Chipotle Aioli ingredients in a small bowl. Serve as topping for tacos, burgers, or as dip for sweet potato frites. Makes 1 cup.

LAST Preheat oven to 450º. Cut potatoes into ½-inch wedges; transfer to a baking sheet and toss with oil. In a small bowl, combine chili powder, paprika, salt and orange zest. Toss oiled potato wedges with spice mixture; spread into a single layer and bake for about 30 minutes, turning occasionally. Serve immediately with Chipotle Aioli for dipping.

ANCHO CORN

This dish turns simple grilled corn into something spectacular.

PLACE indoor
PREP TIME 10 minutes
COOK TIME 30 minutes
YIELD 6 servings

2 teaspoons chili powder
1 teaspoon cumin
1 teaspoon paprika
1 teaspoon salt
½ teaspoon black pepper
4 ears fresh corn, with husks
½ cup feta cheese, crumbled
1 lime, cut into 4 wedges
Olive oil

FIRST In a small bowl, combine chili powder, cumin, paprika, salt and pepper. Set aside.

NEXT Preheat grill to high. Pull back husks of corn, but do not detach. Remove silk and replace husks; soak ears in cold water for 10 minutes. Place corn on the grill; close the lid and cook for 12 minutes, turning occasionally, until kernels begin to soften and husks start to blacken.

LAST Remove corn from grill; allow to cool, then pull back husks. Brush on olive oil, then sprinkle the rub generously on each ear of corn, coating all sides. Top each with feta cheese and serve with lime wedges.

MUSTARD HERB POTATO SALAD

Light vinaigrettes are delicious on potato salads and, because they keep well in the refrigerator, can always be made ahead of time.

PLACE indoor
PREP TIME 10 minutes
COOK TIME 15 minutes
YIELD 6 servings

SALAD
2 pounds Yukon Gold potatoes,
   cut into 1-inch cubes
¾ cup chopped celery
3 tablespoons fresh chopped parsley
½ cup sliced scallions
¼ cup roughly chopped fresh basil

VINAIGRETTE
1 tablespoon Dijon mustard
grated zest of 2 lemons
3 tablespoons champagne or
   white wine vinegar
⅓ cup olive oil

FIRST Place potatoes in a large pot; cover with cold water and add 1 teaspoon salt. Bring to a boil and cook potatoes about 15 minutes, or until fork tender. Drain and place cooked potatoes in a large bowl; add celery, parsley and scallions. Toss well.

LAST In a small bowl, combine mustard, lemon zest, vinegar and oil; whisk until combined. Season to taste with salt and pepper. Pour vinaigrette over potato mixture and gently toss. (Dressing can be added up to two hours before serving.) Toss in fresh basil just before serving; serve warm or at room temperature.

CHIPOTLE MASHED SWEET POTATOES

The chipotle peppers in this recipe give traditional sweet potatoes a twist.
You can easily adjust the heat by adding more or fewer chilies.

PLACE indoor
PREP TIME 10 minutes
COOK TIME 15 minutes
YIELD 4 servings

1½ pounds sweet potatoes,
  peeled and cut into 1-inch pieces
2 tablespoons brown sugar
3 tablespoons milk
1 tablespoon butter
1½ tablespoons chipotle peppers
  in adobo sauce, finely chopped

FIRST Cook potatoes in boiling salted water for 15 minutes, or until tender. Drain and place in a large bowl.

LAST Mash potatoes with a potato masher or fork until smooth. Stir in brown sugar, milk, butter and chipotle peppers. Season to taste with salt and serve.

MOROCCAN COUSCOUS

The key to making couscous that's full of flavor is to season the cooking liquid.
Use chicken stock instead of water, then flavor with herbs and spices.

PLACE indoor
PREP TIME 5 minutes
COOK TIME 5 minutes
YIELD 4 servings

2 cups chicken or vegetable stock
¼ teaspoon ginger powder
¼ teaspoon cinnamon
¼ teaspoon cumin
1½ cups couscous
½ cup pecans, chopped
½ cup dried apricots, chopped

FIRST In a medium saucepan, bring stock to a boil. Add ginger, cinnamon, cumin and couscous; stir to combine. Remove from heat and let sit 5 minutes.

LAST Fluff with a fork, then stir in pecans and apricots.

SMOKED TOMATO AND BASIL PASTA

This pasta makes a wonderful side dish to simple grilled chicken,
but you can double the recipe, add some grilled shrimp
and serve it as a main course, too.

PLACE indoor/outdoor
PREP TIME 10 minutes
COOK TIME 15 minutes
YIELD 4 servings

1 pint cherry tomatoes
1 tablespoon olive oil
2 cloves garlic, minced
1 teaspoon salt
6 ounces thin spaghetti
2 tablespoons olive oil
¼ cup grated Parmesan
¼ cup fresh basil, cut into thin strips
1 15-inch alder grilling plank, soaked
Grill basket for cooking

FIRST Preheat grill to medium-low heat. In a medium bowl, toss tomatoes with olive oil, garlic and salt. Place plank on grill; close lid and heat 3 minutes. Using tongs, turn plank over and put grill basket on the heated side. Spoon tomatoes into basket; close lid and cook 10 minutes, or until tomatoes begin to blister. Remove plank and tomatoes from grill; set aside.

LAST In a large pot of boiling salted water, cook spaghetti until al dente. Drain pasta and place in a large bowl. Toss with olive oil, basil and cheese; season with salt and pepper. Serve with extra cheese, if desired.

NOTE To make indoors, roast tomatoes on a baking sheet covered with parchment 15 minutes at 350°.

BLACK BEAN CAKES

This side dish is the perfect complement to planked tacos.
It's crispy on the outside without being fried
and can make a good vegetarian entrée.

PLACE indoor
PREP TIME 15 minutes
COOK TIME 10 minutes
YIELD 5 servings

2 teaspoons olive oil
1 cup chopped onion
3 cloves garlic, minced
1 cup chopped green bell pepper
2 teaspoons ground cumin
2 teaspoons chili powder
2 15-ounce cans black beans,
    rinsed and drained
1 egg, lightly beaten
1 cup plain bread crumbs
1 cup grated sweet potato
Sour cream, lime wedges and
    lime zest for garnish

FIRST Preheat oven to 500°. Heat oil in a medium skillet over medium heat. Sauté onions and garlic 3 minutes; add bell pepper and continue cooking an additional 3 minutes, or until onions are tender. Stir in cumin and chili powder; set aside.

NEXT Add beans to a large bowl and mash with a large fork or a potato masher, leaving some of the beans whole. Stir in onion mixture, egg, bread crumbs and potato; season generously with salt and pepper. Shape mixture into equal-size patties and place on a baking sheet coated with cooking spray.

LAST Bake in oven 7 minutes, or until crispy. Using a spatula, carefully turn cakes and continue cooking for an additional 3 minutes, or until second side is crispy. To serve, squeeze with fresh lime juice and top with sour cream and lime zest.

SIMPLE ROASTED POTATOES

Although this is a simple dish, it's the perfect complement to many grilled foods.
Yukon Gold potatoes have a delicious buttery flavor, but
you can also use red or fingerling varieties.

PLACE indoor
PREP TIME 5 minutes
COOK TIME 25 minutes
YIELD 4 servings

4 cups Yukon Gold potatoes, quartered
1 tablespoon olive oil
2 cloves minced garlic
2 teaspoons fresh rosemary,
   finely chopped
½ teaspoon kosher salt

FIRST Preheat your oven to 450°. In a large bowl, toss potatoes, oil, garlic, rosemary and salt. Spread in a single layer on a cookie sheet lightly sprayed with oil.

LAST Roast 25 minutes, or until potatoes begin to brown and are fork tender. Season to taste with salt and pepper.

NOTE Get creative with this dish by adding other fresh flavors, such as:

LEMON-MINT POTATOES Omit rosemary and toss potatoes with 2 tablespoons fresh mint and a little lemon juice just before serving.

PARMESAN-CRUSTED POTATOES Sprinkle potatoes with ¼ cup finely grated Parmesan before roasting.

COLORFUL POTATO SALAD Substitute rosemary for thyme and toss hot potatoes with baby spinach or arugula leaves, lemon juice, olive oil and cherry tomato halves.

CHEESE POLENTA

I always keep good-quality corn meal in my freezer so I can prepare
this dish in a snap. Use whatever cheese best matches
the rest of your meal — cheddar, Parmesan, even blue cheese.

PLACE indoor
PREP TIME 5 minutes
COOK TIME 25 minutes
YIELD 4 servings

2 cups chicken broth
2 cups water
1 cup stone-ground cornmeal
1 teaspoon kosher salt
½ cup cubed Fontina cheese

FIRST In a medium saucepan, bring chicken broth and water to a boil over high heat. Whisk constantly, slowly pouring cornmeal into the hot liquid. Stir in salt. Lower the heat and cover.

LAST Cook polenta at a gentle simmer, stirring frequently, until creamy and not grainy, about 25 minutes. Remove polenta from heat, stir in the cheese and serve.

SUMMER SQUASH, ZUCCHINI, FETA AND MINT SALAD

This side dish is light and refreshing, and doesn't require any cooking at all.

PLACE indoor
PREP TIME 5 minutes
YIELD 4 servings

2 small squash, sliced into thin rounds
2 small zucchini, sliced into thin rounds
2 tablespoons fresh lemon juice
2 tablespoons olive oil
¼ cup chopped mint leaves
3 ounces feta cheese, crumbled

FIRST In a large bowl, combine squash, zucchini, lemon juice and olive oil.

LAST Toss with fresh mint and feta cheese; season with salt and pepper, and serve immediately.

CHAPTER SIX | Desserts

SIMPLE FUDGE CAKES

This is a favorite dessert. It's extra gooey and rich if you undercook it just a little.

PLACE indoor
PREP TIME 15 minutes
COOK TIME 30 minutes
YIELD 16 servings

4 ounces unsweetened chocolate, roughly chopped
1 cup butter (2 sticks)
2 cups sugar
4 eggs
1 cup flour
½ teaspoon baking powder
1 teaspoon vanilla
¾ cup chopped pecans (optional)
Powdered sugar for garnish

FIRST Preheat oven to 325° and lightly grease a 9x12 pan.

NEXT Place chocolate and butter in a large heat-proof bowl; set over a sauce pan of simmering water. Stir occasionally, heating until smooth, about 5 minutes. In a large mixing bowl, combine eggs, flour and vanilla; add chocolate mixture and stir in nuts, if desired.

LAST Transfer batter to greased pan; bake 30 minutes or until a small knife inserted into the center comes out with a few crumbs attached. Top with powdered sugar.

PROSECCO AND SORBET FLOAT

Soda shop taste with a touch of class.
This delicious dessert satisfies your craving with style.

PLACE indoor
PREP TIME 5 minutes
YIELD 4 servings

2 cups fruit sorbet
2 cups Prosecco or sparkling wine

FIRST Using an ice cream scoop, spoon ½ cup sorbet into 4 stemmed glasses.

LAST Top each with ½ cup sparkling wine, or more if desired.

NOTE You can make this a kid-friendly dessert by substituting sparkling grape juice for the wine.

WATERMELON BASIL GRANITA

Two of the season's best flavors make this light dessert the perfect end to a summertime meal. Try substituting fresh mint for the basil, too.

PLACE indoor
PREP TIME 20 minutes
FREEZE TIME 3 hours
YIELD 6 servings

⅓ cup sugar
¼ cup packed fresh basil leaves
5 cups watermelon cubes
2 tablespoons lime juice
Fresh basil sprigs for garnish

FIRST Bring sugar and 1 cup water to a simmer in a small saucepan over medium-low heat, stirring until sugar has dissolved. Remove from heat and stir in basil. Let stand 15 minutes; drain through a fine sieve, discarding basil, and set aside.

NEXT In a food processor or blender, purée the watermelon until smooth. Add sugar syrup and lime juice; pulse until combined.

LAST Transfer mixture to a 9x13 metal baking dish. Chill in freezer until edges are frozen, about 1½ hours. Remove from freezer and, using fork, break up crystals every 30 minutes until entire mixture is frozen and crystallized. Spoon granita into serving bowls and garnish with fresh basil.

NOTE Alternatively, freeze overnight until solid. Cut mixture into chunks and transfer to food processor. Blend until mixture is the texture of sorbet.

CRANBERRY AND WHITE CHOCOLATE CHIP COOKIES

A favorite of kids and adults alike, this is a different approach to the traditional chocolate chip cookie. A hint of orange zest gives it an extra burst of flavor.

PLACE indoor
PREP TIME 15 minutes
COOK TIME 10 minutes
YIELD 4 dozen

2¼ cups flour
1 teaspoon baking soda
½ teaspoon salt
1 teaspoon cinnamon
¾ cup butter, softened
¾ cup sugar
¾ cup brown sugar
2 eggs
1½ teaspoons vanilla
2 teaspoons orange zest
1½ cups white chocolate chips
¾ cup chopped pecans
¾ cup dried cranberries

FIRST Preheat oven to 350°. In a medium bowl, combine flour, soda, salt and cinnamon. Set aside.

NEXT Using an electric mixer, beat butter and sugars at medium speed until light and fluffy. Add eggs, vanilla and orange zest; continue beating until well blended. Set mixer at low speed and slowly add flour mixture until incorporated. Stir in white chocolate chips, pecans and cranberries with a rubber spatula.

LAST Drop by heaping tablespoons onto a lightly greased baking sheet. Bake 10 to 12 minutes or until done. Transfer cookies to wire rack to cool.

JEWEL'S FRUIT COBBLER

Jewel, a wonderful Southern cook, was a huge part of my life while growing up.
She always made the most delicious "cobbage," as she called it.
I didn't realize how easy it was to make until I got old enough to cook.

PLACE indoor
PREP TIME 10 minutes
COOK TIME 25 minutes
YIELD 8 servings

4 tablespoons butter
¾ cup self-rising flour
¾ cup milk
¾ cup sugar
1 teaspoon vanilla
3½ cups fresh peaches, peeled and sliced
1 cup fresh or frozen blueberries
2 tablespoons sugar

FIRST Preheat oven to 350°. Put butter in a 9 x 13 glass baking dish; bake until butter is melted. Set aside.

NEXT In a medium bowl, combine flour, milk, ¾ cup sugar and vanilla. In a separate bowl, toss peaches, blueberries and remaining 2 tablespoons sugar.

LAST Pour batter into dish over melted butter, but do not stir. Spoon fruit over batter along with ½ cup fruit juice from bottom of bowl. (Discard any extra juice.) Do not stir. Bake 25 minutes, or until crust browns.

NOTE Use 3½ cups of any type of fresh fruit.

APPLE TARTE TATIN

Any type of apple works for this quick and easy dessert,
and you can make it with regular pie dough, too.

PLACE indoor
PREP TIME 10 minutes
COOK TIME 25 minutes
YIELD 6 servings

4 tablespoons butter
¼ cup sugar
1 teaspoon ground ginger
4 medium apples, peeled, cored
  and cut into eighths
1 12-inch piece of puff pastry, thawed

FIRST Preheat oven to 400°. Melt butter in a 9- or 10-inch cast-iron skillet (or any oven-safe pan) over medium-high heat; add sugar. Gently stir until sugar starts to turn brown, about 3 to 5 minutes. Be careful not to burn the sugar, as it will continue to cook in the hot pan. Turn heat down to low and stir in ground ginger.

NEXT Arrange the apples in the skillet in a circular pattern. Cook for an additional 3 to 5 minutes. Cover the skillet with puff pastry, folding any extra inside the skillet.

LAST Place the skillet in the oven and bake 20 to 25 minutes, or until the pastry is puffed and golden brown. Remove tarte from the oven and let cool, about 5 minutes. Place a serving dish on top of the skillet and turn it upside down; the tarte should gently fall out of the skillet. Serve warm.

CHOCOLATE SORBET

Sure to satisfy anyone's craving for chocolate, this dessert is light at the same time.
For a splash of color, garnish this sorbet with fresh raspberries.

PLACE indoor
PREP TIME 10 minutes
FREEZE TIME 2 hours
YIELD 6 servings

1 cup sugar
2 teaspoons lemon juice
¼ cup cold water
2 cups hot water
⅔ cup unsweetened cocoa powder
½ teaspoon ground cinnamon
½ teaspoon vanilla extract
Pinch of salt

FIRST In a medium saucepan, combine sugar, lemon juice and ¼ cup of cold water. Set on medium heat, stirring occasionally, until sugar has dissolved. Raise heat and boil, washing down sides of pan with a pastry brush dipped in cold water from time to time. Allow the sugar to cook, swirling occasionally, until the syrup reaches a deep golden caramel, about 5 minutes. Remove caramel from the heat.

NEXT Add the hot water carefully to the caramel; stir to dissolve. Whisk in cocoa powder, cinnamon, vanilla and salt. Set aside to cool, whisking occasionally.

LAST Once the mixture has cooled, freeze in an ice cream maker according to manufacturer's directions. Transfer to an airtight container and freeze at least two hours before serving.

CAPPUCCINO POTS DE CRÈME

Your guests will think you spent all day making this delicious dessert.
And because the individual servings keep well in the refrigerator,
you can make them a day or two in advance.

PLACE indoor
PREP TIME 20 minutes
COOK TIME 40 minutes
YIELD 5 servings

1 cup half-and-half
3 ounces semisweet chocolate, chopped
¼ cup strong coffee
¼ cup sugar
¼ teaspoon vanilla
3 egg yolks
Whipped cream (optional)

FIRST Preheat oven to 350°. Place egg yolks in a large bowl and set aside.

NEXT Put half-and-half and chocolate in a large heat-proof bowl; set over a saucepan of simmering water. Stir until chocolate is melted. Add coffee, sugar and vanilla; continue cooking until mixture is smooth. Whisk ¼ of the chocolate mixture into egg yolks, then slowly whisk in remaining chocolate mixture until combined.

LAST Strain chocolate mixture through a fine sieve and divide among 5 small ramekins. Place ramekins in a 9x13 baking pan; fill with warm water until it reaches halfway up the sides. Cover with foil and bake 40 minutes, or until a toothpick inserted in the middle comes out clean. Serve with whipped cream, if desired.

CEDAR-WRAPPED APPLES WITH WALNUT TOPPING

This apple dessert is comfort food any time of year, but you can also substitute with other fresh fruits, such as peaches and pears, when they're in season.

PLACE indoor/outdoor
PREP TIME 10 minutes
COOK TIME 8 minutes
YIELD 4 servings

2 tablespoons brown sugar
2 tablespoons butter, melted
1 tablespoon flour
½ teaspoon cinnamon
a pinch of nutmeg
½ cup walnuts, toasted
¼ cup raisins
1 large Granny Smith apple,
    cored and cut into ¼-inch wedges
4 cedar papers, soaked
Vanilla ice cream or brie cheese

FIRST Preheat grill pan or grill to medium heat. In a small bowl, combine sugar, butter, flour and spices; stir in walnuts and raisins. Set aside.

NEXT Divide apple wedges among 4 papers and top each with ¼ of walnut mixture. Fold edges of paper in, overlapping apple mixture, and secure with cotton string.

LAST Grill 4 minutes per side or until apples are tender. Serve with vanilla ice cream or warm brie.

FROZEN LEMON MERINGUE PIE

This is a refreshing spin on the classic lemon pie.
To save a little time, you can also use a purchased graham cracker crust.

PLACE indoor
PREP TIME 25 minutes + chill
COOK TIME 1 minute
YIELD 8 servings

CRUST
½ cup pecans
¾ cup graham cracker crumbs
¼ cup sugar
5 tablespoons butter, melted

FILLING
2 cups lemon sorbet, softened
2 cups vanilla ice cream, softened
5 egg whites
¼ teaspoon salt
½ cup plus 1 tablespoon sugar
¼ teaspoon lemon juice

FIRST In a food processor, chop pecans until finely ground. Add graham cracker crumbs and sugar. While the processor is running, pour melted butter through the feed tube. Process the mixture until just combined. Press mixture into the bottom of a 9- or 10-inch pie pan. Chill until set, about one hour.

NEXT Using an electric mixer, combine softened ice cream and sorbet; beat until mixture is smooth and well combined. Spoon ice cream mixture into pie plate and freeze until firm, about 4 hours.

LAST Place egg whites, salt and lemon juice in a bowl; beat until stiff peaks form. While beating, gradually add sugar until well combined. Spread mixture on top of pie filling and broil for one minute, or until meringue is lightly brown. Serve immediately or return to freezer.

CHAPTER SEVEN | Grilling Guide

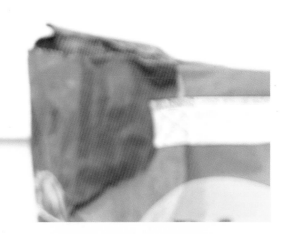

Because a special occasion calls for a special meal,
even when that occasion is a Tuesday.

SIMPLE GRILLING TIPS

Grilling is the go-to technique for weeknight meals. It's simple, fast, and requires virtually no cleanup. Whether you're a grilling guru or a novice, this section is sure to be an indispensable reference that will guide you through the recipes in this book.

CREATING A TWO-LEVEL FIRE

When preparing any of the recipes in this book, it is best to build a two-level fire, which allows your grill to have both a hot and cool spot. Having two different temperatures is an easy way to regulate cooking. It will allow you to sear meat on the hot spot and let you finish cooking on the cool one. If the grill is hot all over, your food will burn. Likewise, if your grill is too cool all over, your food won't achieve that delicious crispy sear.

HERE'S HOW

GAS GRILL   Turn all burners to high; close the lid and heat 15 minutes, or until the grill reaches about 450°. Once heated, leave one burner on high and turn the other down to medium low.

CHARCOAL GRILL   Light the charcoal; heat until the grill reaches about 450°. Build a two-level fire by stacking most of the hot coals on one side and spreading a single layer of coals on the other. Set grate on grill; close lid and heat 5 minutes.

GRILLING TEMPERATURES

The recipes in this book call for specific temperatures (what the thermometer should read on the grill's hot spot when using a two-level fire). To determine the temperature, use a grill thermometer. Or to use the hand test, hold your outstretched palm 4 to 5 inches above the grill grate, then count the number of seconds you can comfortably leave it there.

USING A THERMOMETER
- HOT: 500°F
- MEDIUM HOT: 450°F
- MEDIUM: 400°F
- MEDIUM LOW: 350°F

HAND TEST
- 1 to 2 seconds, the grill is HOT
- 3 to 4 seconds, the grill is MEDIUM HOT
- 5 seconds, the grill is MEDIUM
- 7 seconds, the grill is MEDIUM LOW

THE BASICS OF PLANK GRILLING

Plank grilling, a concept that has been around for centuries, has only recently been rediscovered. As Native Americans found, the process seasons food with an aromatic smoky flavor.

The technique plays right into today's demand for casual, health-conscious lifestyles. And the bonus? Plank cooking is easy. Even the most novice griller can master this process. With our simple suggestions and helpful hints, you'll soon be preparing perfectly planked food.

WHY PLANK GRILLING?

GREAT FLAVOR WITH EASE
Have you ever tried to turn a delicate piece of fish on the grill, only to have it break apart into tiny pieces? One of the benefits of plank grilling is that foods don't have to be turned. Fish and other lean proteins stay moist and delicious.

A HEALTHY APPROACH
When plank grilling, foods cook in their own juices. No additional fats or oils are needed to enhance the flavor or prevent it from sticking.

EASY CLEAN-UP
By cooking food directly on a plank, there are no pots or pans to clean up. Even better, the planks — food and all — can go directly from the grill to the table, which makes for a show-stopping presentation.

WHERE TO FIND PLANKS

Until recently, grilling planks were difficult to find. But due to their fast-growing popularity, they're now readily available in a variety of sizes and woods types. Look for grilling planks in the seafood or grilling sections of your local supermarket or at specialty gourmet shops. *(See Resource Guide, page 184)*

COMMON PLANK TYPES

WESTERN RED CEDAR

FLAVOR   Robust, sweet, and smoky

COMPLEMENTS   Cedar is the best complement to salmon, as well as heartier meats such as beef, pork and lamb. It also pairs well with duck and wild game.

NOTE   *If using cedar, be sure the planks you use are 100% Western Red Cedar. Certain types of cedar — such as white, inland or aromatic varieties — can give food bitter or perfume-like flavors.*

ALDER

FLAVOR   Subtle smoky flavor that is slightly sweet and nutty, with a hint of vanilla

COMPLEMENTS   Alder pairs well with salmon as well as more delicate fare such as shrimp, scallops, halibut, snapper and other white fish. Its light smoky flavor also works well with lean pork, chicken, fruits and vegetables.

MAPLE

FLAVOR   Mild smoky flavor that is smooth, sweet and buttery

COMPLEMENTS   Maple is delicious with pork and poultry. The buttery-rich flavor also pairs well with lighter seafood, fruit, cheese and vegetables.

OAK

FLAVOR   Aged smoky flavor that is similar to that of Southern barbecue

COMPLEMENTS   Oak gives beef, pork and chicken a wonderful smoky finish. It's a great choice for stronger-flavored meats such as wild game.

CAUTION   *Use only untreated, 100% natural wood for plank grilling. **Never** use leftover decking or lumber, because it is often treated with pesticides and chemicals.*

WHAT YOU'LL NEED TO GET PLANKING

GRILLING PLANK made specifically for cooking

SOAKING PAN or the kitchen sink; I like to use a disposable aluminum lasagna or roasting pan

HEAVY OBJECT such as a wine bottle or pot to keep the plank submerged under water

GAS OR CHARCOAL GRILL

GRILLING OR OVEN THERMOMETER if your grill is not equipped with a built-in thermometer

BOTTLE OF WATER for potential flare-ups

TONGS AND A LARGE SPATULA for plank handling

COOKIE SHEET OR HEAT-PROOF PLATTER for moving plank from the grill to the table

SAFETY PRECAUTIONS

- Never leave a grill unattended.
- Because planking creates smoke, be careful when opening the grill lid to keep from getting smoke in your eyes.
- Soak your plank at least one hour and up to 24 hours.
- Never use treated wood.
- Keep a spray bottle filled with water nearby in case of flare-ups.
- Always remove the plank from the grill after food is done. Even if the grill is off, the plank can flare up.
- Check foods periodically during the plank-grilling process but do not open the grill too quickly, because oxygen feeds fire.

PLANK GRILLING CAN BE DONE ON GAS OR CHARCOAL GRILLS

Either type requires a thermometer to monitor your temperature. If your grill is not equipped with one simply use a standard oven thermometer, placing it directly on the grill grates.

Generally, gas grills should be heated to medium-low (350°) for plank grilling. For beginning plank grillers, gas grills are easier to monitor and control the temperature.

Charcoal grills also work well for plank grilling. Because a properly built charcoal fire gets much hotter than a gas fire, a two-level fire is recommended for plank grilling. Mound charcoal on one side of the grill for cooking at hotter temperatures and use a single layer of charcoal on the other half for lower-temperature grilling. This technique will give you room to move the plank to a lower temperature if it gets too hot during the cooking process.

HOW TO PLANK GRILL

SOAK

- Soak the plank, completely submerged, in water for at least one hour. Use a heavy pot or wine bottle as a weight.
- Be creative with your soaking liquids. Try adding flavors such as beer, wine, fruit juice or even bourbon to the soaking water.
- Place the plank in water before leaving for work and it will be ready to go when it is time to prepare dinner.

HEAT

- Heat a gas or charcoal grill to medium low (350°). Place the soaked plank directly on the hot grill grates; close the lid and allow the plank to heat for 2 to 3 minutes, or until a light smoke develops.
- Preheating the planks is important because it allows the plank to begin releasing smoke and flavor.

SMOKE

- Once the plank is preheated, turn it over with a pair of tongs and place your food directly on the heated side of the plank. Close the lid of the grill and allow the food to cook until desired doneness.
- The plank should generate a light smoke, which adds flavor to foods. If the amount of smoke starts to become heavy, reduce the grill temperature or move the plank away from hot coals (toward the edge of the grill) and continue cooking.
- Occasionally check the plank by slowly opening the grill. Keep a bottle of water nearby to extinguish any flames that may occur.

EAT

- Once your food is done, remove it and the plank from the grill with tongs. Because the bottom of the plank will be extremely hot, place it on a cookie sheet or a heat-proof platter.
- Foods will continue to cook once they are removed from the grill. For that reason, you may want to remove meat and seafood before they are completely done to avoid overcooking.
- The beauty of plank grilling is that you can take the entire plank straight to the dinner table. It's a simple, delicious, fun and foolproof way of cooking.

TIPS FOR PLANKING YOUR FAVORITE FOODS

CHICKEN, PORK AND BEEF

1 Heat grill to medium hot or about 450°.

2 Sear meats first. Searing meats directly on the grill, before planking, will seal in juices and produce a lightly charred appearance. Lightly oil grill grates (to prevent the food from sticking); place the meat on the grill and sear approximately 60 seconds per side. Remove meat from grill and set aside.

NOTE *Some people oil their foods directly and then place them on the grill. I prefer to oil the grill grates, so there's not a significant amount of fat added to the food. Roll a paper towel into a ball and, holding it with tongs, dip in oil and rub the grill grates. Be sure that the grates are clean before cooking; use a wire brush to clean them after the grill has heated for a few minutes.*

3 Reduce your grill temperature to medium-low heat, or 350°. If you are using charcoal, use the cooler side of the grill for plank cooking.

4 Preheat plank according to directions.

5 Transfer seared meats to plank.

6 Remove meat from the grill when it is 5 to 10 degrees shy of the desired internal temperature. The temperature will continue to rise for several minutes after the meat has been removed from the heat source.

	RARE	MEDIUM-RARE	MEDIUM	WELL-DONE
RED MEAT (BEEF, LAMB, VEAL)	125°	130°	140°	160°
PORK	*	*	145°	160°
CHICKEN (DARK MEAT)	*	*	*	165°
CHICKEN (WHITE MEAT)	*	*	*	165°

SEAFOOD

Plank grilling is the perfect method for cooking seafood. There is no turning needed, nor will seafood break apart and fall through the grill. Fish takes a few minutes longer to cook on a plank, but the results are delicious, moist and tender.

CARRYOVER COOKING The heat from the plank will continue to cook the fish, even after it has been removed from the grill. If you prefer tuna or salmon medium-rare, remove the fish-topped plank from the grill a minute or two before it is done to your liking.

SHELLFISH Shrimp and scallops cook quickly. Be sure that your plank is giving off a little smoke before placing shellfish on it. Otherwise, the food will be done before the flavor can be imparted.

DONENESS Check for doneness by nicking the flesh with a paring knife. Most fish should be opaque at the center, although tuna and salmon can be cooked until just translucent in the center.

VEGETABLES

Vegetables are delicious when cooked on alder and maple planks; the subtle smoky flavors make everyday vegetables unique.

GRILLING BASKETS Because smaller items such as cherry tomatoes, new potatoes and diced vegetables tend to roll off of a plank, use a grilling basket placed directly on top of it. This will also allow you to periodically toss the vegetables while cooking.

BLANCHING For tender, quick cooking, blanch potatoes and firmer vegetables such as green beans, carrots and broccoli before placing on a grilling plank.

FINISHING TOUCHES For a quick side dish, toss planked vegetables and potatoes with olive oil and:
  Cheese — feta, goat cheese, blue cheese or Parmesan
  Chopped herbs — parsley, thyme, marjoram or basil
  Chopped nuts — pecans, walnuts, pine nuts or hazelnuts

COOKING WITH CEDAR PAPERS

Like plank grilling, cedar papers impart a delicate smoke flavor into foods. The soaked papers are first wrapped around seafood, meat, vegetables, fruits and even cheese, and then grilled. The papers can be used on an outdoor gas or charcoal grill, in the oven, on a grill pan or even on an electric grill. Whichever way you choose, the results will be juicy and flavorful.

Cooking with cedar papers allows you to get creative. Top your seafood and meat with fresh herbs, citrus slices, vegetables and flavored butters. The foods will steam to perfection with a subtle, smoky flavor.

SOAK

Submerge papers in water-filled shallow dish for 10 minutes, using a small bottle or glass to weigh them down.

HEAT

Place fish, vegetables, fruit or cheese in the center of a soaked paper, parallel to the wood grain. Fold the paper's edges toward each other until they overlap; secure with cotton string, if necessary. Preheat grill or oven to 400°, or an indoor grill pan to medium high.

SMOKE

GRILL OR GRILL PAN Place cedar roll seam side down on the grill and cook 4 minutes per side, or until done to your liking.
OVEN Place cedar roll seam side down on a baking sheet; bake approximately 10 minutes, or until done to your liking.

EAT

Serve cedar-wrapped foods straight to the dinner table, then sit back and enjoy the compliments.

RESOURCES

GRILLING PLANKS AND PAPERS

FIRE & FLAVOR GRILLING CO.   866-728-8332   www.fireandflavor.com

CAST IRON GRILL PANS AND COATED ENAMEL COOKWARE

LODGE MANUFACTURING COMPANY   423-837-7181   www.lodgemfg.com

GRILLS

BIG GREEN EGG   770-938-9394   www.biggreenegg.com

FRESH GEORGIA PEACHES AND PECANS

LANE SOUTHERN ORCHARDS   800-27-PEACH   www.lanepacking.com

PEARSON FARM   888-423-7374   www.pearsonfarm.com

TAYLOR ORCHARDS (peaches only)   478-847-4186   www.taylororchards.com

GOAT CHEESE

SWEET GRASS DAIRY   229-227-0752   www.sweetgrassdairy.com

COACH FARM   518-398-5325   www.coachfarm.com

WILD SALMON

WILD ALASKA SALMON AND SEAFOOD CO.   866-648-WILD   www.wildalaskasalmonandseafood.com

CONVERSION CHART

FLUID OUNCES	MEASUREMENT	MEASUREMENT	MILLILITERS
½ ounce	3 teaspoons	1 tablespoon	14.8
2 ounces	4 tablespoons	¼ cup	59.2
2⅔ ounces	5 tablespoons + 1 teaspoon	⅓ cup	78.9
4 ounces	8 tablespoons	½ cup	118.4
8 ounces	16 tablespoons	1 cup	236.8
16 ounces	2 cups	1 pint	473.6
32 ounces	4 cups	2 pints/1 quart	947.2
128 ounces	16 cups	8 pints/4 quarts	3.79 liters

SIMPLE SUBSTITUTIONS

You may not always have every ingredient you need on hand, but before you run back out to the store, here are some easy to find substitutions that can save you the trip.

CAYENNE PEPPER   Hot pepper sauce or chili paste

EGG (1 LARGE)   2 egg whites or ¼ cup egg substitute

GARLIC (1 CLOVE)   ¼ teaspoon garlic powder

GOAT CHEESE   Feta cheese

HERBS, FRESH (1 TABLESPOON)   1 teaspoon dried

MUSTARD, PREPARED (1 TABLESPOON)   1 teaspoon dried mustard with 2 tablespoons white wine vinegar or water

SHALLOTS   Scallions, white part only, or mild white onion

SHERRY VINEGAR   Balsamic vinegar

SELF-RISING FLOUR (1 CUP)   1 cup plain flour plus 1½ teaspoons baking powder and ½ teaspoon salt

SOUR CREAM   Yogurt

INDEX

ACKNOWLEDGEMENTS

I would like to express my sincere gratitude to all of the people who helped make this book a reality. Thanks to everyone for your time and incredibly hard work.

Thanks to Erica George Dines, an amazing photographer, for making all of the shots so beautiful.

Thanks to Heather Paper for her creative writing skills and attention to fine detail. Her enthusiasm for this book always shines even under the toughest working conditions.

Thanks to Dan Cleveland for providing access to a beautiful garden for our photo shoot—and his endless advice on my own garden.

Thanks to Angie Mosier for her fabulous styling on our entertaining shoot. She is an incredibly talented stylist with endless ideas.

Thanks, especially, to Erica George Dines and Gill Autrey, for making all of the photo shoots such fun. While we each had our own role—Erica, the photographer; Gill, the art director; and myself, the food stylist—everyone pitched in to make each shot spectacular. The creative ideas that bounced back and forth often made for long hours but nobody seemed to mind, knowing that the results would be amazing.

NOTES